BRAND VANDALS

KT-416-803

BRAND VANDALS

Reputation Wreckers
and How to Build Better Defences

Steve Earl and Stephen Waddington

B L O O M S B U R Y
LONDON • NEW DELHI • NEW YORK • SYDNEY

First published in Great Britain 2013

Copyright © Steve Earl and Stephen Waddington, 2013

Bloomsbury Publishing Plc
50 Bedford Square
London
WC1B 3DP

www.bloomsbury.com

Bloomsbury Publishing
London, New Delhi, New York and Sydney

All rights reserved; no part of this publication may be reproduced, stored
in a retrieval system, or transmitted by any means, electronic, mechanical, photocopying or otherwise, without the prior written permission of
the Publisher.

No responsibility for loss caused to any individual or organisation acting
or refraining from action as a result of the material in this publication can
be accepted by Bloomsbury Publishing or the authors.

A CIP record for this book is available from the British Library.

ISBN: 9-781-4729-0520-8

10 9 8 7 6 5 4 3 2 1

Design by Fiona Pike, Pike Design, Winchester
Typeset by Hewer Text UK Ltd, Edinburgh
Printed in the United Kingdom by CPI Group (UK) Ltd, Croydon CR0 4YY

We dedicate this book to the wonderful individuals
who have the greatest influence on our lives;
our personal team of brand vandals.

Saskia, Alfie, Ivan and Sarra Earl

Dan, Ellie, Freya and Katie Waddington

CONTENTS

ABOUT THE AUTHORS

Steve Earl

Steve Earl has been at the forefront of progressive public relations, advising on news management, integrated storytelling and earning the hard yards of reputation through potent content for the best part of 20 years. He has been a news journalist, global public relations consultant, agency entrepreneur and media pundit. And apart from the journalist bit, he still is.

Earl is European managing director for Zeno Group, advising clients in consumer, technology and healthcare PR as he leads the regional growth of the agency and continues to develop its fearless approach to brand and reputation management across conventional, social and owned media around the world.

He is co-author of *Brand Anarchy: Managing Corporate Reputation* (Bloomsbury, 2012) the provocative, bestselling guide to managing reputation, and is a regular blogger for *PRWeek* in the UK.

Earl trained as a news journalist before following a career in public relations. He has co-founded and run two award-winning public relations agencies with co-author Stephen Waddington; Rainier PR in 1998, and Speed in 2009. He has helped brands such as The Associated Press, BT, Cisco, *The Economist*, IBM, Tesco and Virgin Media to manage their reputations.

In 2001, when he was young, he was named *PRWeek*'s Best Young PR Professional. His teams have won The Holmes Report's Best UK Agency to Work For awards three times.

He is married with three young children, lives in north London and can spot a stray apostrophe at a staggering distance. He is a member of The Wine Society and British Cycling, though he tries to keep those affiliations separate. He knows practically everything about bikes, apart from how to keep them clean.

Stephen Waddington

Stephen Waddington has earned a reputation as a public relations moderniser, thought-leader and consumer engagement advocate through senior roles during the last 20 years as a public relations consultant, author and journalist.

Stephen is European digital and social media director for Ketchum, advising clients throughout Europe as well as those assisted globally by the agency from North America, Asia and Latin America.

He is President-Elect of the CIPR, the professional body for the UK public relations industry. He currently serves on the CIPR Executive Board and is Chair of the Institute's Policy and Campaigns Committee and its Social Media Panel.

Stephen understands how the media landscape works online and offline and champions best practice as a writer, conference speaker and award-winning blogger.

He is co-author of *Brand Anarchy: Managing Corporate Reputation* (Bloomsbury, 2012) and editor and contributor to *Share This: The Social Media Handbook for PR Professionals – from the CIPR* (Wiley, July 2012).

Stephen originally trained as a journalist before following a career in public relations. He has co-founded and run two award-winning public relations agencies; Rainier PR in 1998, and Speed in 2009. He has helped brands such as The Associated Press, Cisco, The Economist, IBM, Tesco and Virgin Media Business to manage their reputations.

He is a Chartered Practitioner and in 2012 received an Outstanding Contribution to Social Media award at the UK Social Media Communications Awards.

Stephen is married with three children and splits his time between work in London and increasingly further afield, and home on a small holding in rural Northumberland.

ACKNOWLEDGEMENTS

There are lots of people who have influenced our thinking during the development of both *Brand Anarchy* and *Brand Vandals*.

In particular we'd like to thank the following people for providing support with the development of *Brand Vandals*.

Darryl Sparey, Will McInnes, Ged Carroll, Howard Walker, Ross Wigham, Dan Howe, Molly Flatt, Andrew Thomas, Rachel Miller, Sarah Pinch, Kate Bosomworth, Ged Carroll, Adam Parker, Steve Rubel, Andrew Grill, Sarah Hall, Joy Stefanicki, Mark Adams, Phillip Sheldrake, Francis Ingham, Gabbi Cahane, Marshall Manson, Jane Wilson, Margaret Clow, Azeem Azhar, Sarah Hall, David Armano, Georgie Cameron, Jonathan Copulsky, James Whatley, Louise Terry, Michael Brito, Charles Bell, Hannah Christian, Katie Elias, Craig Mersky, Dan Howarth, Nic Seton, Jas Dhaliwal, David Gallagher, Robert Phillips, David Phillips, Philip Young, Anthony Mayfield and Mat Morrison.

We'd thoroughly recommend you look them up online if you're seeking thought-provoking conversation.

INTRODUCTION

Thanks for buying *Brand Vandals*. It's our second book, written in response to the reaction to our first book, *Brand Anarchy*.

The feedback on *Brand Anarchy* took us both by surprise. It has received positive write-ups in industry trade magazines and has been recommended as a text for students of brand communications, marketing and public relations throughout Western Europe. We are called on to speak about the issues raised in *Brand Anarchy* at conferences and events, comment in traditional media and consult with organisations about how they tackle the issues raised in the book.

Whenever we are asked to speak about *Brand Anarchy* people want to know two things: firstly, how bad can it get; can you share some examples? and secondly, is there a solution?

Brand Vandals is a follow-up book that aims to answer both of these questions. It is a book in two parts: the first half, written by Stephen Waddington, examines the damage that Internet-empowered individuals can cause organisations. The second half, written by Steve Earl, proposes some answers for the future of organisational communications. In fact the final chapter tells you how you might get cracking in just 90 days.

Since the publication of *Brand Anarchy* we've gone our separate ways professionally, leaving Speed, the agency that we founded in 2009. After 14 years of working together and building two progressive and influential public relations agencies, we have both moved to roles at world-leading public relations firms.

Steve Earl is building European operations and advising clients on how to build greater value through converged media for Zeno Group, a sister company of Edelman, while Stephen Waddington is plying his trade at Ketchum, growing the agency and helping its global clients get to grips with digital and social media.

The book has been written using many of the techniques that we advocate. A content plan was developed, working with Bloomsbury Publishing, and then drafts were shared in real time using Internet-based services. We aim to practice what we preach.

We hope that *Brand Vandals* leaves you feeling empowered and ready to deal with brand vandals. There really has never been a more exciting time to work in organisational communications, if you can keep a sense of perspective and know the ropes of a new media landscape.

Finally, make sure you look us up on Twitter, our preferred social media weapon of choice. Steve is @mynameisearl and Stephen is @wadds. We'll both keep our eyes on #BrandVandals for your thoughts.

Steve Earl and Stephen Waddington
London, UK
October 2013

SECTION 1 – THE RISE OF BRAND VANDALS

STEPHEN WADDINGTON

CHAPTER 1

IT CUTS BOTH WAYS

> Media has become a two-way weapon. Nobody can control it. It's anarchy. #BrandVandals

The Internet gives brand vandals ready access to the brands they target and harm, and new ways to do so. But the canny organisation is one that realises it cuts both ways – becoming closer to your audience can give you better protection.

The Internet and media have brought about fundamental shifts in the way that organisations communicate. We weren't exaggerating when we described the situation as anarchy in our first book. We were called out for using *Brand Anarchy* as the title by Alastair Campbell, the self-proclaimed Downing Street spin doctor, during Prime Minister Tony Blair's premiership. Campbell famously operated a command and control style of media relations, seemingly maintaining an iron grip on the media and the government's reputation. He said of *Brand Anarchy* that we were exaggerating to make a point and grab headlines.[1] That's praise that we happily accept from one of the most fearsome organisational communicators of our generation. We've no doubt that it helped drive sales. Thank you, Alastair.

The biggest change in media and organisational communications in the last 60 years is that communication between an organisation and its audiences can no longer be one-way. It never should have been but organisations have managed the flow of information to their audiences, often using the media as

---

1 And there's more: *Brand Anarchy* heads for a second reprint, *Two-Way Street*, Stephen Waddington, http://wadds.co.uk/2012/10/25/and-theres-more-brand-anarchy-heads-for-second-reprint/ (25 October 2013)

a proxy for engagement. It's much easier to deal with a handful of journalists than manage thousands of direct relationships. Thanks to the Internet everyone has a voice and the opportunity to call out an organisation. Anyone can publicly criticise and be a brand vandal. But then they always could. Consumers have shared their views of organisations whenever one or more people have gathered together in coffee shops, pubs, school playgrounds, bathrooms or bedrooms. The difference now is that everyone is able to share this opinion for anyone else in the world to see and to share acts of brand vandalism. And guess what? They do.

Without being overly dramatic, the Internet has democratised elites and flattened society. It is forcing individuals and organisations to be more accountable than ever before. In 2000, the *Cluetrain Manifesto*[2] foretold that markets were conversations. Now anyone with a mobile phone or tablet with access to the Internet can publish their point of view about an organisation. If they are upset they can write negative comments and become a brand vandal. These views can be shared thanks to social media or discovered thanks to search engines. Communication between an organisation and its audience has become two-way, or a conversation, to use the modern day parlance of the Web, exactly as *Cluetrain* predicted. Organisations can no longer avoid these conversations. And why would they? These same organisations spend vast sums in a bid to engage with their prospects, customers and stakeholders. Thanks to the Internet they can now find anyone talking about their business or the markets in which they operate. Not all organisations want to listen to these conversations and some claim to be listening but

2 Christopher Locke, Doc Searls and David Weinberger.*The Cluetrain Manifesto*. Financial Times Series – Perseus Books Group (17 May 2000)

aren't at all. But then these conversations don't always make for easy listening.

Organisations used to operate under the belief that they could control how a message was communicated to an audience. Much of the organisational discipline of corporate communications has been built on this premise. In reality, organisations can plan their public relations activity and carefully craft messages and content but total control has never been possible. A message will only resonate with an audience if the audience believes it to be sincere and authentic. It will be shared, discussed and debated. We're back to the conversations that take place in coffee shops, pubs, school playgrounds, bathrooms and bedrooms.

Today, thanks to the Internet these conversations also now take place beyond physical boundaries and locations. They are passed on through social networks such as Google +, Facebook and Twitter. Each individual with their social and digital connections is the gateway to other networks. Once a message hits a network any notion of control is immediately lost and as we're set to discover, brand vandals have the opportunity to wreak havoc with an organisation's reputation.

New models of organisational communications over a cup of tea

In their book *Online Public Relations* David Phillips and Philip Young[3] state that Internet technologies have disintermediated not only organisational communications but the entire value chain of commerce. It's a bold statement but we believe that it

---

3 David Phillips and Philip Young. *Online Public Relations: A Practical Guide to Developing an Online Strategy in the World of Social Media*. Kogan Page US (3 May 2009)

is spot on. 'The context in which an organisation can thrive is rapidly moving from its ability to create traditional relationships with publics to its ability to do this in an online world, and mostly via third parties that are beyond its control. [...] The presence of information and messages about organisations is spread by and through many devices and platforms that transmit and receive information. Distribution is effected by web crawlers and search engines.'

You can test Phillips' and Young's hypothesis for yourself very simply in the time that it takes to make a cup of tea or coffee. In fact head to Google, or any other search engine, and type in the name of your favourite brand of tea or coffee. We're PG Tips drinkers. A Google search query returns 29 million pages. The PG Tips Facebook page has around 1,000 likes and 100 comments per post and Twitter returns a tweet every 30 seconds from someone enjoying a cup of tea. PG Tips has created less than one per cent of this content. The simple fact that has been laid bare by the Internet and social forms of media is that an organisation does not own the conversation around its products or services. A tea manufacturer can only hope to influence what is written about it by how it communicates and the relationships that it builds with its audiences. This is the narrative of social media and it is causing upheaval for organisational communications. It's an incredibly exciting time.

The point, well made, by Phillips and Young is that the vast majority of content on the Web about an organisation is not under its control and the opportunity for engagement is limited. In fact it's often not possible for an organisation to monitor all the mentions of it online let alone interact in a meaningful way. Herein is the opportunity for the brand vandal to call out and criticise a brand and vandalise its reputation. The social web is made up of conversations on blogs, forums and social networks such as Facebook and Twitter, accessible in moments in response to a search query. They put the public firmly in control of the reputation of an organisation, placing the audience at the heart of the conversation.

There ain't no stopping it now

The genie is very firmly out of the bottle and there is no going back. The Internet has seen phenomenal growth in the last 10 years with more than two billion people being connected online. The two technology drivers have been broadband networks and mobile. In the Western hemisphere networks are being upgraded from copper to high-speed fibre. In Asia and the BRIC economies countries are leapfrogging directly to fibre. Mobile connectivity is following a similar cycle as networks are upgraded to 4G or built from the ground up in markets. Here's a defining signpost for the future: 2013 will be the year that the Internet goes mobile as the number of consumer mobile devices such as smartphones and tablets overtakes personal computers, according to data from Silicon Valley venture capital firm Kleiner Perkins Caufield & Byer (KPCB).[4] Access to the Internet is becoming truly ubiquitous. You'd better ensure that your website is responsive to different browser environments if it isn't already.

Google is building its business with the expectation that around three billion new consumers will join the Web in the next seven years according to European boss, Matt Brittin, speaking at an Omnicom conference in January 2013. Brittin explains that real life is coming to the Web. 'There are currently 2.4 billion people on the Web. It will be twice that before the

4 Kleiner Perkins Caufield & Byer. *2012 Internet Trends*. http://www.kpcb.com/insights/2012-Internet-trends-update (December 2012)

end of the decade. I carry the Internet in my pocket. This will be the experience that consumers will have of the Internet in the future,' he said waving a sub-$100 Android device in the air that he'd purchased on a recent trip to Asia.

In the late 1990s, when consumer Internet connectivity first became a mainstream consumer product, the Internet was a destination. It was a place that you visited using a personal computer and browser. Now, as Brittin observes, we carry the Internet around in our pockets thanks to smartphone devices and burgeoning mobile networks. The shift to mobile marks a notable behaviour change for consumers. This was significant as it removed the shackle of wires. Consumers could browse the Internet on the move, which has added an additional layer of information and communication to life. It's a layer that transcends government and commerce and democratises society. The next surge of growth is already in sight as electronic products such as cars and white consumer goods are connected to the Internet to share information and data.

People are using the Internet for a huge variety of applications ranging from entertainment to events and from commerce to communications. But the single largest category on the Internet is social media. According to Tom Standage, digital editor at *The Economist*, social media can no longer be dismissed as a passing Internet fad. Social networks may rise and fall in popularity but the medium is here to stay for some fairly fundamental reasons. Speaking at the Omnicom event Standage names three reasons for our enthusiasm for social media and its wholesale adoption, namely biological, historical and cultural.

Human beings, explains Standage, have a larger neocortex than any other animal. This is the part of the brain that manages sensory perception, motor commands, spatial reasoning and language. It accounts for 85 per cent of the volume of the brain. In an article in 1992 in the *Journal of Human Evolution*,[5] Richard Dunbar, a British anthropologist based at the University of Liverpool's School of Biological Sciences, found that this enabled human beings to protect themselves by maintaining a relationship in a large group. Social media, it seems, is scratching a biological itch according to Standage. Dunbar's work gave rise to the Dunbar number, a theory that asserts that human beings can only maintain between 100 and 230 one-on-one relationships, with a commonly assigned value of 150.

The second of Standage's explanations for the popularity of social media is historical. Social media has decentralised communications. Again he cites the democratisation of media. Authority no longer lies with traditional media owners; now anyone can publish content and reach an audience. Standage uses the metaphor of the 18th-century coffee house. Here, individual titles and authority were left at the door. Thinkers shared their thoughts and ideas via the media of a pamphlet. Coffee fuelled discussion and debate. Today, pamphlets have been replaced by blogs, tweets and Facebook posts.

The third and final of Standage's explanations for the rise of social media is its cultural role in people's lives. The time spent engaged in social media is increasing. In fact it's no longer really possible to separate what activity online is social as now everything is social. The adoption of technology as a means of driving social activities is increasing across the generations and is becoming deeply embedded in people's lives. You need look no further than the frequency with which people in your network log on to Facebook or Twitter for evidence.

---

5 'Neocortex size as a constraint on group size in primates.' *Journal of Human Evolution*, http://www.sciencedirect.com/science/article/pii/004724849290 081J (Vol. 22, Issue 6, June 1992, pp. 469–493)

Our appetite and adoption of social media has been truly astonishing. When radio was invented in the 1900s it took nearly 40 years to reach an audience of 50 million. Television reached the same audience within 13 years. The Apple iPod took three years. Facebook took a matter of months. The inescapable fact is that technology accelerates the pace of human interaction and it's a trend that is only set to increase. The future of social media is likely to involve more networks than fewer. A second tier of networks is developing alongside the main networks such as Facebook, Google+, LinkedIn and Twitter. These networks such as Instagram, Pinterest and Vine overlay an application on social interaction and are each, in turn, creating new communities and building niche audiences.

The relationship between users and networks isn't always straightforward. Networks must play the delicate balancing game between providing a service to users and being a valuable media product for advertisers. You see this issue played out each time a network makes a change to its terms and conditions such as when Facebook changed its newsfeed algorithm in November 2012 so that only a fifth of users received organic posts in their newsfeed or when Twitter ceased to display Instagram images as media content the following month. Social networking in 2013 is a lot like Internet access was in 1998 with walled gardens preventing access to the wider Internet beyond. Then it was AOL and Compuserve; now it's Facebook and Twitter. Our view is that the social networks who fail to open-up will very quickly alienate their community and they will move. This is something that has played out time and time again in the past with previous iterations of technology. There's a harsh irony of social networks. If users choose to reject a network and shift their attention elsewhere it is incredibly easy to tell your network where you are going. Friendster and MySpace both discovered this to their cost.

Always-on and the tension between work and play

Organisations are playing catch-up with the speed of technological change in every sense. The simple fact is that most people have a better experience of technology in their personal lives than they are allowed to in their professional lives. It's a truism that was highlighted by Dave Coplin in a session at Social Media Week in London in September 2012.[6] Coplin is an information technology consultant turned thought leader and evangelist who works for Microsoft's search engine business. 'We go from these incredible experiences – shopping online, playing games, communicating with friends – and then we cross the threshold next morning when we go into work and we get greeted with something typically along the lines of "computer says no",' he said. 'Computer says no' was the catchphrase of an unhelpful receptionist played by David Walliams in the UK hit comedy series *Little Britain*. It has entered human parlance to describe a situation whereby someone in authority uses a computer to hide their own incompetence or plain rudeness. People typically walk around with a smartphone or two in their pocket that is more powerful and better connected than the one on their desk at work.

Meanwhile some organisations prevent their employees from using social media by blocking specific sites. Management believes that allowing access would either hinder productivity or that by somehow ignoring the conversations that are taking place across social channels they will be silenced. Coplin is characteristically damning. 'If you think that people will waste

6   Dave Coplin. *FIR Speakers and Speeches*., Microsoft, on Future Forward at #SMWB2B, For Immediate Release, http://forimmediaterelease.biz/index.php?/weblog/comments/fir_speakers_and_speeches_dave_coplin_microsoft_on_future_forward_at_smwb2b (26 September 2012)

their time engaged in social media then you need to frisk people for newspapers and Sudoku books when they walk in in the morning as the same principle applies,' he says. 'Ignoring conversations is to ignore your prospects, your customers and your market. You need to realise how many of your customers and consumers live and exist in those channels. The reality is that there is an easy way to make this happen,' said Coplin. His message is clear. Ultimately we have to get back to the place where the experience we have of technology in our personal lives is matched by what we can do in our professional lives.

Managing democratic communication

There are two possible reactions to social media within an organisation: social media as a bolt-on channel; and social media as a strategic platform for engagement with your audience. There is a third option, of course, which is to ignore social media completely and hand your reputation over to the brand vandals. Fortunately, this is no longer a route that many organisations are taking. In using social media as a bolt-on channel, an organisation transfers the communication techniques that it has used with its traditional audiences – typically the media – and supplements them with a sprinkling of social media. You can spot these organisations everyday on Facebook or Twitter spewing out content with little or no attempt at engagement. In contrast, the strategic approach to social media recognises that this platform offers an organisation the chance to put future prospects and customers at the heart of its business. This is the shift towards social business.

In 2013 if a company creates a social channel as a marketing vehicle it is inevitable that consumers will use it as a mechanism for customer service and sales. It's no secret that the fastest way to resolve a customer service issue is to complain noisily via Twitter. If you haven't seen this consumer behaviour before, check out the Twitter profiles and conversations of any of the mobile, broadband or train providers. We have plenty of examples of such brand vandalism to share with you throughout the book. The simple fact is that it's a lot simpler for consumers to complain via Twitter than to visit a retail store or deal with an offshore call centre.

The willingness for consumers to embrace social media is one of the reasons that many sectors, such as retail banking, have been slow. The fact is that they simply wouldn't be able to cope with the demand from customers seeking to engage directly. For brands it's an issue of customer service as well as reputation. Organisations have to quickly integrate their social channels with other operational parts of the business, giving rise to the social business. But consumers also need to temper their expectations. Re-engineering businesses so that they put social communication at their core will take time. These changes may be driven by technology but ultimately they are cultural and organisational and will take several generations to play out.

The social opportunity for organisations

Precise is a £30 million media monitoring company that has built an intelligence business based on providing brands with clippings and insight of their mentions in print, radio and television. Its customers are public relations agencies and communications departments of corporate, government and third sector organisations. Precise's stock trade is coverage and analysis reports examining sentiment and share of voice that are delivered to the desks of customers at the start of each day. As media changes Precise has been quick to change its business model. It has spotted a bigger opportunity to become the eyes and ears of an organisation, watching and listening to the conversations that are taking place in the market. I caught up with business development director at Precise, Darryl Sparey, to find out more.

Sparey is an old friend. We grew up in the media and public relations industry together. We share a passion for the North East of England and its people, which has manifested itself in us both pairing up with partners from Newcastle. When we meet it's at the Breakfast Club in Spitalfields, London, a bustling café-cum-diner that serves city workers and East London creative types. 'Our opportunity is to move down the corporate corridor knocking on the doors of other departments within an organisation. There isn't an area of a business that social media doesn't touch. It's a continuous barometer of market opinion. Not listening to these conversations is effectively admitting you don't care what your customers or other stakeholders are saying,' said Sparey.

Sparey makes a compelling case for social media listening and watching within every department of an organisation. Over bacon and eggs, he takes me on a journey through an organisation, explaining Precise's value proposition along the way. 'The most obvious area of a business affected by social media is customer services. For service providers, particularly utilities and telecommunications, major supermarkets and consumer-facing financial services we have seen a huge increase in the volumes of service-related Facebook posts and tweets over the past couple of years,' he said.

Recent analysis undertaken by Precise for a retail bank identified 6,500 pieces of social media content that specifically related to customer service issues or queries, out of a total of over 26,000 in one month. Service providers have, or are currently creating, social media customer services teams to respond to queries from online channels around the clock. 'We have found that by having analysts look at this type of content to spot trends and patterns, we're also able to help clients iden-tify causes of customer service issues that may be quick and easy to rectify, and deal with those issues before they reach a much larger audience,' said Sparey

Another department that is enthusiastically embracing social media, according to Sparey, is sales, in particular business-to-business sales. 'Most modern sales people will now follow their prospective companies and individuals they're talking to on Twitter. It's an invaluable way of knowing what your prospects are thinking right now. You only have to look at the investment Salesforce is making in social media with the acquisition of Radian6 to know that this is an important area. Klout scores, LinkedIn and Twitter are all now featured out of the box within Salesforce. For the majority of our clients, we will provide monitoring services not just for a company, but for their competitors as well – when someone comments negatively about a competitor of yours, for a sales person that can be a great opportunity, with the right approach, to introduce your-self,' said Sparey.

Within human resources, as usage of social media by employees has increased, so has the need to track what employees are saying. In 2010 IBM had 17,000 internal blogs and almost 200,000 employees on LinkedIn[7]. Whilst IBM publishes a directory of its bloggers online, as well as its social media policy, many other organisations are struggling to keep track of which of its employees are going online and saying something about their business or their market. Monitoring and understanding which of your employees is active online is

---

7   Social Media Examiner, *How IBM uses social media to spur employee innovation*, http://www.socialmediaexaminer.com/how-ibm-uses-social-media-to-spur-employee-innovation/ (2 February 2010)

very important. There's an obvious positive communications angle to this – if you can identify people with genuine enthusiasm for something, with an engaged audience, they can be the very best advocates for your business externally.

Then there's product development. Social media has created unique opportunities for so-called crowd-sourcing product development. Lego has a platform called ReBrick where it encourages users to upload images of their own Lego creations. The most popular are then put into mass production. Whilst few brands have customer creativity as a core value of their brand, or the worldwide brand recognition that Lego has, there are many examples, according to Sparey, where Precise have worked with clients to help them to identify a new market, a new audience or a new opportunity for their products and services through rigorous analysis of social content about themselves and their competitors. Consumption habits are of particular interest, so the real-time nature of Twitter makes this a rich source of information for understanding what consumers are interested in right now.

Even the finance department is getting in on the act. 'We know of one company who is using social media tracking, in connection with other data, to predict company failures and bankruptcies. In this way, finance departments may be better able to understand and quantify risks of potential bad debts. There is also a financial communications benefit. Precise has briefed finance directors of some of its publicly listed clients by analysing the comments on investors' blogs, forums and other social media to anticipate the questions that may come from the floor at shareholder meetings,' said Sparey.

The White House as media

Organisations throughout the world are reskilling and reorganising how they deal with the social web and prioritising different forms of media as they impact on different areas of business. Some, such as the White House, are moving a lot quicker than others and are reaping the benefits. President Barrack Obama swept to power in the US in 2008 thanks to his campaign team's use of social media for campaigning and fundraising. In 2007 Obama was a little-known senator from Illinois yet by November 2008 he was the first African-American to win the election and become the 44th US President.

Much of Obama's success resulted from the groundswell he created using social media to raise money and develop a network of empowered volunteers. The campaign was underpinned by a social network called my.barrackobama.com allowing individuals to connect with one another and participate directly in the campaign. My.barrackobama.com enabled the President-to-be and his team to solicit input from supporters. More than two million signed up as activists and advocates. Notably, Obama modified key elements of the election policy on healthcare as a result of debate within the community. The Obama campaign in 2008 and the re-election campaign in 2012 are likely to have a huge influence on the way that political election campaigns will be run in the future. They demonstrated the potential of technology to engage people and bring about a direct call to action at a grassroots level.

But it hasn't stopped there. The Obama administration has continued to use social media as a means of direct engagement with the US electorate throughout the administration's time in the White House. This has seen social forms of media prioritised ahead of traditional media, much to the chagrin of the traditional Washington press corp. During a Google+ hangout in February

2012 Obama claimed that his administration was the most transparent in history. Media in Washington don't share the President's enthusiasm. The tension results from the White House becoming a publisher of its own content on its own terms. The new media channels favoured by the administration are blogs, Facebook, Flickr, Google+, Twitter and the White House's own Web TV channel. Content is carefully orchestrated using the White House website as a hub. Media interviews are granted to network anchors or local television stations but no such luck for Washington reporters at *The New York Times* or *The Washington Post*. The White House has implemented a strategy of owned social media channels combined with relatively soft editorial targets compared with the Washington media. The result has firmly tipped the balance of power between the media and the White House in favour of the White House.

In defence of public relations

The gain for the public relations industry from the changing media landscape is a loss for traditional media. In an era when brands are able to communicate directly with their audience, with the public relations industry facilitating that process, the role of traditional media is much diminished. The media has the public relations industry in its line of fire; the relationship between the two communities has always been feisty.

Ian Burrell, media journalist at *The Independent*, a UK newspaper, cited the growth of the public relations industry as bad for journalism in a critical article[8]. Burrell says that

---

8 Ian Burrell, 'Why news that PRs outnumber hacks is bad for journalism.' *The Independent*, http://www.independent.co.uk/news/media/opinion/ian-burrell-why-news-that-prs-outnumber-hacks-is-bad-for-journalism-8281319.html (5 November 2012)

the balance of power in the communications triangle between organisations, the media and publics has shifted over the last 20 years. According to Burrell's research the latest headcount of journalists in the UK stands at 40,000 whereas the public relations industry numbers 60,000. 'Any big story now invariably develops into a credibility contest between the reporter and the communications team of the organisation under fire, with social media becoming a battlefield of damage limitation,' he says.

This is the same argument advanced by City of London University journalism professor, Roy Greenslade[9]. He goes further, claiming that the growth of public relations combined with the decline of journalism is an affront to democracy. Greenslade cites a statistic from Nick Davies' excellent book *Flat Earth News* and data from the Holmes Report. We reached a place in 2008, according to Davies, where there are more public relations practitioners than journalists in the UK. The Holmes Report records global revenue for the public relations industry at more than $10 billion.

The simple fact is that media organisations employ less journalists than they did in the past. The Internet has broken the shackles of deadline, page count and schedule. It has made the distribution cost of content almost zero and has provided search and social mechanisms to aid discovery of content. Anyone with an Internet connection can become a brand vandal and voice, providing a contrary filter to corporate content. Journalists have been supplemented by publics noisily voicing their comment and opinion. For its part the public relations

9   Roy Greenslade, 'More PRs and fewer journalists threatens democracy.' *The Guardian*, http://www.guardian.co.uk/media/greenslade/2012/oct/04/ marketingandpr-pressandpublishing (4 October 2012)

industry, supplemented by increasing numbers of former journalists, myself included, is helping organisations engage with publics in a two-way dialogue. That dialogue is seldom easy. You can see the evidence of organisations that get it wrong day in and day out on corporate websites, blogs, Facebook, Google + and Twitter. This is forcing organisations to be more open and transparent, not less so as Burrell and Greenslade suggest.

The communications and public relations function is under scrutiny like never before, called out by the self-same critical publics. This is a story of changing business models fuelled by the Internet. It strengthens the democratic process, not weakens it. Our view is that the public relations industry must cease being introspective and define its value to organisations as the reputational and relationship adviser. It must confidently assert its contribution to the broader economy if it is to earn the place that it deserves as a professional services discipline.

As organisations recognise the opportunity that new forms of media provide to engage directly with publics and the potential reputational hit from brand vandals if they don't, the industry has the opportunity to take the lead role in the communication between an organisation and its audiences. It's a work in progress as the shifts in media continue and it will more than likely take a generation to work through. In the meantime the debate about who owns social media is a distraction. Markets may be started by conversation but ultimately they are created and nurtured through action. Public relations practitioners need to be brave and modernise their practices if they want to grasp this opportunity.

The new attention game

There's a turf war taking place between advertising, media buying, public relations and digital agencies. I don't use that term lightly; it is a war. The battles are taking place in pitches and the reorganisation of communications and marketing departments day in, day out. The battle lines are being drawn by media change and audience consumption and the positions that advertising, public relations and digital assert. In many instances the lines between the disciplines are blurring to the extent that it is not possible to tell one from the other. If a county council posts an editorial news update in its Facebook newsfeed and then pays to promote it to ensure that all its followers see the message, is that advertising? If a retail brand works with a peer analytics firm, such as Klout, Kred or PeerIndex to identify the key influencers in its niche and then pays the company to manage an influencer campaign on its behalf, is that public relations?

The threat to public relations taking the lead is its failure to adapt to new forms of media as quickly as other disciplines. We've been here before. In 1998 a company called Google launched with the purpose of enabling Internet users to find the most relevant content online. Its vision of organising the world's information and making it universally accessible and useful has remained consistent for more than 14 years. The rest, as they say, is history. Google created an opportunity for a new industry to help organisations create content and build relationships online. By the end of 2013, according to econsultancy[10], that industry was set to be worth $26.8 billion. It's called search engine optimisation and is a growing segment of the burgeoning digital industry.

The advertising industry isn't backwards at coming forwards, either. In January 2012 the UK Advertising Association published an independent report by Deloitte called *Advertising*

---

10 Econsultancy. *SEMPO State of Search Marketing Report,* http:// econsultancy.com/uk/reports/sempo-state-of-search (September 2012)

Pays that claimed that the advertising industry contributed £100 billion to the UK economy. That's the sort of headline that makes government and business sit up and listen. In fact it's the sort of headline that gets the attention of the UK Treasury. 'At a time when advertiser-funded media models continue to face pressure, particularly following huge spending cuts by government and when advertising budgets are being squeezed, this was a timely reminder to government on the value of the advertising industry,' said Jane Wilson, CEO, CIPR. *Advertising Pays* sets out to quantify and qualify the economic effects of the £16 billion spent on advertising in the UK every year[11]. It sought to examine the return on investment for advertising spend, claiming that for every £1 spent on advertising the economy grows by £6. Deloitte's research is the start of a conversation between the advertising industry and a CEO in the public or private sector. The public relations industry simply doesn't have the same weaponry.

The 2011 *PRWeek*/PRCA Census concluded that the public relations industry was worth £7.5 billion to the UK economy[12]. Our advertising colleagues have outsmarted us by taking on the macro contribution of advertising to the economy rather than a micro view. It would be great to see a piece of third-party research on behalf of the public relations industry that made this broader connection. I had a conversation a couple of years ago with public relations consultant and author, Mark Borkowski, about the difference between the advertising and public relations industries and which was likely to win the

---

11 Jane Wilson. *Articulating the value of public relations*, http://thatwilsonthing. com/2013/02/04/articulating-the-value-of-public-relations-and-a-necessary-culture-shift/ (4 February 2012)

12 'UK PR industry worth £7.5 billion data from PR Census 2011 reveals.' *PRWeek*, http://www.prweek.com/uk/news/1080127 (14 July 2011)

attention of the boardroom as media fragmented. Exactly the same conversation is taking place every day in bars and restaurants across the world from Soho, London to Madison Avenue, New York. Borkowski is a plain-speaking practitioner who has built world-class agencies and advised leading brands, so his opinion is always worth seeking out. His view is that the advertising industry simply has more swagger.

It's an issue of confidence but it's also a matter of agility.

The advertising industry isn't waiting for permission to become the adviser to brands as they seek to engage in conversations with their audiences. It has been quick to recognise how its strengths in planning, creativity and production can be used in the new media environment. It also benefits from a business model that enables agile teams to be built based on individuals' skills to meet a client's requirements. The public relations industry, for its part, arguably has the most potent proposition for organisations. It has always worked in the editorial environment, listening and crafting a narrative, to enable organisations to build their reputation by earning attention rather than buying it. But the industry needs to be brave enough to align its business model from the hierarchical structures of old with the new challenges that organisations face.

CHAPTER 2

FROM ANARCHY TO TERROR

Is social media mobilising the angry mob or is it merely an outlet for people who moan and bitch? #BrandVandals

If you spend your day glued to Facebook or Twitter – and we're well aware that there are those that do – it would be easy to believe that social media was set to bring about revolution as people noisily share their passions and anger. Of course, there are examples where online conversations have been the catalyst for significant change. But the impact of social media on society isn't actually that different to any other prior form of media. This is an issue that has exercised me for some time. Don't get me wrong, there is no doubt that it has played a significant role in situations such as the Arab Spring in Tunisia and surrounding countries, and the riots in England in Summer 2011, but we've yet to see the impact of the radical transparency that science fiction writer David Brin envisaged in his book *The Transparent Society* in 1999[13].

Brin claimed that there is no equaliser greater than knowledge and he predicted that social and organisation transparency between citizen and state would bring about greater equality. He predicted that the erosion of privacy by low-cost surveillance and database technology would be matched by full disclosure of organisations and governments, creating new organisation structures that would compensate for the lost personal privacy. The argument for information democracy goes something like this: I know about you. You know about

13 David Brin. 'The Transparent Society: Will Technology Force Us to Choose Between Privacy and Freedom?' Basic Books, a member of the Perseus Group (16 April 1999)

me. Corporations and the government are watching us. But we're also watching them. You know my secrets but I know your secrets. We're still waiting for Brin's vision of information utopia. The relationship is never equal; it is always weighted in favour of the state.

US computer specialist and writer Bruce Schneier debunked the notion of a transparent society in an article in *Wired* in 2008 claiming that it ignores the chasm between those elites with power and those who access power.[14] 'You cannot evaluate the value of privacy and disclosure unless you account for the relative power levels of the discloser and the disclosee,' said Schneier. 'If I disclose information to you, your power with respect to me increases. One way to address this power imbalance is for you to similarly disclose information to me. We both have less privacy, but the balance of power is maintained. This mechanism fails utterly if you and I have different power levels to begin with,' he added.

Delicate balance of trust between consumers and Internet services

The National Security Agency (NSA) is a US intelligence agency based in Fort Meade, Maryland, responsible for analysing data intelligence from overseas. The work of the NSA went on unreported until June 2013 when a former security contractor called Edward Snowden leaked information about a programme called PRISM to *The Guardian* newspaper in the UK. According to Snowden, PRISM gathers text, photos and video content from a number of US Internet services and social networks including AOL, Apple, Facebook, Google, Yahoo! and YouTube, amongst

---

14 Bruce Schneier. 'The Myth of the 'Transparent Society.', *Wired*, http://www.wired.com/politics/security/commentary/securitymatters/2008/03/securitymatters_0306 (6 March 2008)

others. Surveillance of US citizens is illegal under the Fourth Amendment of the US Constitution. It is only allowed where there are grounds for suspicion and then it must be legally sanctioned by the courts.

The US administration was quick to reassure American citizens that they had nothing to fear because the work of the NSA only targets foreigners. It's a sensitive topic that pits civil liberties and the freedom of the individual against the US government's desire to protect the US from terrorist attacks. In a US Senate hearing following *The Guardian* leak, NSA boss Keith Alexander defended the practice of Internet surveillance, claiming that it had 'smashed dozens of terrorist plots'. Inevitably, information about the scale of PRISM or outcomes from the programme is hard to come by because it relates to national security. According to information leaked by Snowden the NSA uses a tool called Boundless Informant to track how much intelligence data is gathered worldwide by the NSA. Charts show that the agency collected almost three billion pieces of intelligence from US computer networks over 39 days through to March 2013.

Data privacy and security is critical to the relationship between technology companies and consumers who are expected to share personal information in exchange for using services for free. The reality of social networks is that if a service is free, you're the product. Consumers continue to use services providing that the value they gain outweighs privacy concerns. If this delicate relationship is breached, consumers will be quick to remove their profiles and accounts and leave social networks and web services. Unsurprisingly the organisations affected have all been quick to issue denials, protesting that they would never share data with a third-party as a matter of course. Facebook's CEO Mark Zuckerberg and Google CEO Larry Page both said that they have never given any government direct access to their servers. The implication is that the

NSA monitors equipment connected to the Internet, replicating and storing information for analysis.

Technology companies will disclose data when legally required to do so, for example in the case of a criminal investigation or at the request of a court. Requests are reviewed by legal teams and considered on an individual account-by-account basis. In a bid to protect their reputation and maintain consumer trust Facebook, Google, Twitter and Microsoft have all asked the US government for permission to publicly disclose instances when they are legally requested to share user data. They all realise that consumer trust is critical to ensuring that consumers continue to use their services. It's a delicate relationship based on trust.

Disconnect: social media versus society

I sought out the view of my long-term friend and former colleague Ged Carroll. We caught up for breakfast at our favourite greasy spoon café, The Stockpot in London's Panton Street, before he headed off to take up a digital marketing role in Hong Kong with Burson Marsteller, one of the world's biggest public relations firms. Carroll found his way into technology because, unlike his fellow peers in the UK in the early 1990s, he had no fear. He learned about computers hands-on because there wasn't any budget for an IT department in many of the early companies where he worked. Five years in industry gave him experience of Macs, mainframes, DEC VAX mini-computers, IBM and SGI UNIX boxes. He got his first email address in 1994. He has blogged about the social impact of digital technologies on his popular blog *renaissance chambara* since 2004.

Carroll now plies his trade helping organisations get to grips with engaging with their markets on the Internet. 'Why,' I asked 'has the social web failed to live up to initial free market expectations?' His response was intriguing and delved back into the origins of democracy itself. The simple fact is that conversation online isn't aligned to the communities which it purports to influence. 'If Facebook or Twitter did reflect society then the Pirate Party would dominate Western governments and state security would be managed by a cabal of the activist and hacking group Anonymous on an IRC (Internet Relay Chat) channel,' joked Carroll.

It's a flippant comment but it makes the point. Carroll believes that to understand the relationship between society and social media you need to look back to Ancient Rome. This was a thriving civilisation that spread from Italy as early as the 8th century BC to become one of the largest empires in the ancient world. Rome was organised along democratic structures that we would recognise today. It was based on a system of annually elected officers and representative assemblies. Debate within the assemblies was robust, brutal, even. The Roman Empire continued to grow and become richer. Life for citizens in ancient Rome was good.

'Bread' and 'circuses' from the Latin *panem et circenses* was the primary concern, as writer Juvenal recorded in the poem *Satires*. These three words characterise the slow decline of the Roman Empire from around 50 BC. The phrase has become a metaphor for universal means of appeasement. If citizens are fed and entertained then political leaders go unchallenged. 'Social media discussion is a modern-day forum of debate by an elite of sorts. The average citizens in the West have access to relatively cheap food and as many television channels and as much Internet access as they can consume. The status quo in society continues unimpeded by the sated mass populace,' said Carroll.

Carroll cites the London Olympics in 2012 as an example of a huge circus, to borrow from *Satires*. I am sure that Tony Blair didn't see the economic restructure coming, but he did see the value of a sated populace when he supported the London bid. 'Undoubtedly, there were some incredible achievements. The event contributed to a brief upsurge in some parts of the UK economy. But it was largely an entertaining distraction, staged by the government, that helped mask three years of decline and the huge shifts taking place as the economy continues to be transformed by technology and globalisation,' said Carroll.

Brand vandalism on a professional scale

'I'm often asked who spends the most on public relations. Who has the biggest communications budget? Who has the highest lobbying bill? Everyone always expects me to say BAE Systems, BP or General Electric. The biggest budgets come not from a listed company investing heavily to protect its corporate reputation but from non-government organisations and pressure groups spending heavily to campaign against an issue or organisations,' said Andrew Thomas, publishing editor, *Communicate* magazine.

Thomas has unique and first-hand insight into the attacks that brands face on their reputation and the steps that they are taking to modernise their communications. We were keen to seek out his view on how corporate organisations are getting to grips with the radical transparency that the Internet has brought about.

'The argument one often hears is that a poor minnow like Greenpeace is a tiny voice against the might of an oil industry giant like BP. Indeed, on paper, Greenpeace spent £37,000 on lobbying in 2011, compared with £5.5 million from BP. And yet Greenpeace exists only as a pressure group. It has no manufacturing base, no line for new product development in its budget. Every penny it spends is effectively spent on communications. And that's not a small amount. In 2011 its budget was £208 million. This is before you also factor in an army of unpaid volunteers, doubling that figure in terms of the labour, skills and expertise they get,' said Thomas.

He goes on to say, 'Now, please don't misunderstand my sentiments. I'm grateful for organisations like Amnesty International, Friends of the Earth and Greenpeace. The work they do is vital in terms of ensuring there is a genuine collective conscience and accountability. Within a democratic capitalist structure pressure groups provide many of the checks and balances needed. However, the sectors on which these NGOs predominantly campaign against have not traditionally needed a public-facing image.'

Here's the issue for organisations. The Internet has turned audiences and organisations inside out, meaning that organisations have no choice but to engage with public audiences. For example, only 20 per cent of oil is destined for cars and petrol stations are predominantly franchise-holders anyway. Mining and weapon manufacturing obviously do not target the consumer and, other than in the US, the pharmaceutical sector is not allowed to reach out to the consumer. However, the growth of the pressure group has, in turn, meant that these non-consumer-facing organisations have had to massively increase their investment on lobbying, corporate public relations and reputation management.

'One of the key issues for companies from these sectors has been the age and dynamism of those attracted to volunteer or work for the pressure groups. It has always been the younger generation that has more time to devote to protest. It is the young, digitally native, wired generation that has joined the wars against the defence companies, the energy sector, the extraction industries and so on,' said Thomas.

'Some of the most memorable campaigns of recent times have been Greenpeace's "Orang-utan's finger" and the Friends of the Earth's "BP rebranded". Two campaigns that were almost impossible for Nestlé or BP to retaliate against without increasing the issues that the campaigns raised. The business community is in constant catch-up mode, as the protesters are able to provide greater numbers and greater understanding of social communications. But it will always be catch-up. The pressure groups will continue to outspend and outsmart the "dirty sectors" because they exist for no other function. If they weren't they wouldn't really be doing their job,' he added.

Culture Shock: Meeting Will McInnes

Will McInnes is more upbeat. He is the founder of Nixon McInnes, a pioneering social business firm. His book *Culture Shock*[15] is a manifesto for the modern networked society. It isn't an easy read because it challenges almost everything that we've learned and know about business but ultimately you'll find little with which to argue. McInnes has learned on the job. His clients at Nixon McInnes have included BBC, Barclays, Channel 4, Cisco, O2, The Foreign & Commonwealth Office and WWF.

McInnes calls for a complete rethink of business to put people and communities back at its heart. It demands a radical overhaul of organisations and financial systems. I challenged McInnes to commit to a timeframe for his vision. He believes that huge schisms are occurring because of transparency and connectedness and that these in turn will force change. 'I swing between wildly optimistic and utter despair. There are plenty of promising signs; some are catastrophic and beyond our control such as the financial crisis or climate change, while there are others where we can have a very direct impact such as how we invest and engage in politics,' said McInnes.

Technology is a consistent, disruptive theme that underpins *Culture Shock*. McInnes spotlights the impact of people who have grown up with technology being hired into senior roles in

15 Will McInnes. *Culture Shock*, John Wiley, (August 2012)

organisations. He cites the example of a retail bank, typically the most traditional of organisations, appointing a technologist to its board, who subsequently spearheaded a disruptive mobile payment system on behalf of a major UK bank.

Darren Foulds joined Barclays as an analyst in 1999 and worked his way through a variety of technology and management roles to become chief operating officer of the retail arm of the bank in 2010. He left that role in the middle of 2011 to lead Barclays Mobile and headed up a mobile payment system, Barclays Pingit, a contactless system that allows current account customers to send and receive cash using their mobiles. 'When an individual with technology in their DNA is appointed to the board of Barclays and then spearheads a product that could fundamentally change how consumers transact you have to recognise that something has changed,' said McInnes.

Ubiquitous Internet connectivity is forcing a change of pace in business. But there are other issues at play. The failure of the banking system, global warming, the Arab Spring and the rise of the BRIC (Brazil, Russia, India and China) economies are driving what McInnes calls an ever-increasing change of velocity in society. But when online communities are seemingly more engaged than ever before it seems that Western political systems are ever more disenfranchised. Voter turnout is at an all-time low. I ask McInnes what needs to change. 'There is an awakening happening fuelled by online discourse. Look at 38 Degrees, Azaaz and Mumsnet ... even Facebook and Twitter. At some point online discussions will bleed into the mainstream. It's already happening as online discussions spill into the media and vice versa. We're at the very beginning. A community such as Wikipedia that has brought about great advancements in education and knowledge sharing will seem trivial in time. It's very early days,' said McInnes.

Real power to the people

38 Degrees is an impressive organisation launched in 2009 in honour of The Body Shop founder Anita Roddick, that works to bring about action in the UK by campaigning on issues. It has grown to become one of the UK's biggest campaigning organisations with more than 850,000 members. The organisation is entirely driven by its members and operates independently of any other organisation, lobbying group or political party. Thirty-eight degrees is the angle at which a build-up of snow in nature will collapse and create an avalanche. 38 Degrees enables people in the UK to act together to create a virtual avalanche for change.

38 Degrees is one of a growing number of organisations around the world such as Avaaz, which operates internationally and on a regional basis, GetUp in Australia and MoveOn in the US. Collectively, these groups mobilise more than nine million people on issues about which their members are passionate. Anyone can become a member of 38 Degrees providing that they share the community's vision of creating a more progressive, better and fairer society. The community is united by shared values: protecting rights, promoting peace, preserving the planet and deepening democracy. It's a laudable vision and it works.

38 Degrees gives UK citizens the opportunity to get involved in politics in a new way. The action of the community makes a real difference. It has helped stop the government's sell-off of ancient forests thanks to a high-profile Save our Forests campaign; it ensured that Donald Trump's plans to build a golf course at the expense of the eviction of the local community were blocked and it persuaded the government to sign up to the European Union Directive on human trafficking.

Members link up, discuss and vote on issues via an online community. 38 Degrees uses a variety of online and offline tactics – such as online petitions, telephone campaigns, events involving stakeholders, such as MPs, and meetings – to bring about change. The community receives some money from charitable trusts including the Isvara Foundation, The Funding Network and the Joseph Rowntree charitable foundation. Beyond that members donate to support either a campaign or action.

The initial idea for a campaign is seeded by members on 38 Degrees' blog, email, Facebook page, Twitter and website. A small team of staff and volunteers find the best ways to have an impact on the issues that have highest priorities to members.

The Save our Forests campaign aimed at blocking the UK government's sell-off of forests across the UK started with a member posting on the 38 Degrees Facebook page. The issue received hundreds of comments directly and via email and so it polled members by email and sought out expert opinion. It moved quickly to launch a petition that engaged tens of thousands of people within a week. Eventually the petition was signed by more than 500,000 people. Within a matter of weeks members contributed to the cost of advertisements in the national media to raise the profile of the campaign. Ministers dropped plans for the forest sell-off.

Spin alive and well: Savile shows need for greater media transparency

Proponents of the social web, myself included, like to think the networked society is a brave new world where transparency is the only option for organisational communications. But for now it simply isn't the case and change is slow. How can you explain the Jimmy Savile scandal that didn't come to light until almost a year after his death? Savile was a popular radio and television celebrity in the UK in the 1970s, 1980s and 1990s. His career followed the rise of broadcast television. He used his popular persona and television profile to raise funds and support numerous charitable causes, notably involving children. After his death, aged 84, allegations of child sex abuse became public, leading the police to believe that he may have been a prolific sex offender.

How was it possible for an individual to abuse so many young people yet maintain such a high media profile? At best, due to its collusion, or at worst, wilful ignorance on the part of the media and the establishment. The story of Savile's behaviour did come out in the end, 12 months after his death, but only because critics of the BBC spotted a weakness in a *Newsnight* story and took the opportunity to attack the corporation. It can't be much comfort for Savile's 300 alleged victims that Scotland Yard, the headquarters of the Metropolitan Police in London, says have come forward.

We learn that rumours of Savile's behaviour have circulated newsrooms for decades. These stories went unreported because Savile was considered untouchable. He was a popular BBC celebrity whose work and good deeds bought silence. This pact was so strong that Savile was able to continue abusing children unreported. Presenting an individual or organisation in the best possible light is the stock trade of media publicists. Stories are the currency of this market. The rules are straightforward. Publicists provide access to individuals or organisations in return for positive press coverage – or silence, in the case of a misdemeanour. The media holds up the relationship for its part to maintain access and ensure a steady flow of stories with which to bait its audience.

Is Savile a one-off from a bygone era, or are similar crimes going unreported because to break the silence would be inconceivable? If it's the latter the inevitable question is, 'How many more Savile-like scandals involving individuals or organisations is the media keeping under wraps?' In 2012 the coalition government in the UK appointed Lord Justice Leveson to lead a public inquiry into the culture, ethics and practices of the UK press following the News International phone hacking scandal that resulted in the closure of the *News of the World*. Relations between the media and the state have never been straightforward in the UK. The Leveson Inquiry is the seventh time in less than seven decades that a report has been commissioned by the government to deal with concerns about the press.

A series of public hearings were held during 2011, when journalists, editors, celebrities and political and business leaders gave evidence into press intrusion and freedom of speech. The Inquiry published the *Leveson Report* in November 2012, which reviewed the general culture and ethics of the British media. It called for a new self-regulatory body, underpinned by legislation, to replace the existing Press Complaints Commission. That remains a work in progress pending legislation but what's also required is greater transparency within the media, government, corporations and publicists to ensure stories such as Savile aren't covered up.

Framed by an algorithm

Search engines increasingly reflect popular opinion and shine a bright light on issues, whether right or wrong. If enough people make a query via a search engine such as Bing or Google the algorithms start to make connections and start serving results, often before you've finished typing in your query, let alone hit enter. This technology is called autocomplete. Dave Coplin, Microsoft UK's director of search, explained how it happened during a session during Social Media Week in London 2012[16].

---

16 Dave Coplin. *FIR Speakers and Speeches*, Microsoft, on Future Forward at #SMWB2B, For Immediate Release, http://forimmediaterelease.biz/index. php?/weblog/comments/fir_speakers_and_speeches_dave_coplin_ microsoft_on_future_forward_at_smwb2b (26 September 2012)

'Let's just say I'm a famous television personality and a media title in the UK decides I've probably been doing something dodgy with my taxes, so "Dave Coplin Tax Dodger" is the headline. The day that article gets published, if I'm popular enough, hundreds of people will type into a search engine "Dave Coplin tax evasion".'

If enough people type that query in, after a while, the algorithm makes a connection between phrases. The next time somebody searches on 'Dave Coplin' the search engine serves 'Dave Coplin tax' as a potential search query. This isn't a fictitious story. It's what happened in June 2012 after *The Times* revealed that comedian Jimmy Carr allegedly used a tax avoidance scheme to minimise his tax liability. Six months later both Bing and Google offered 'Jimmy Carr tax' as an option when you type the comedian's name into the search field. This situation arises whenever there is speculation about an individual or organisation in the media and consumers head to Google to find out more information about the story. Autocomplete suggestions are made by Google's algorithm in real time based on repetitive search queries. Legal appeal to Google is the only possible solution.

Whenever machines are used to automate an editorial process without human intervention there is opportunity for unintended consequences inflicting brand vandalism. Amazon faced criticism when a seller promoted t-shirts with offensive phrases promoting rape and violence. US clothing company Solid Gold Bomb used an algorithm to source slogans, added them onto t-shirts with the iconic World War II poster phrase 'Keep Calm and...' As a result t-shirts with phrases including 'Keep Calm and Knife Her', 'Keep Calm and Punch her' appeared in the Solid Gold Bomb shop on Amazon. The artwork was generated automatically. The t-shirts didn't actually exist until the request was received at which time the wording would be printed on demand as customers placed their orders.

Solid Gold Bomb founder Michael Fowler explained that the company had created a computer algorithm to generate parody t-shirts after a trademark had been granted for the phrase, 'Keep Calm and Carry On.' It's something that clothing companies frequently do. 'My response to this was to create a large-scale release of parodies and rely on both computer-based dictionaries and online educational resources, such as verb lists,' explained Fowler.

'As the volume of combinations of words, slogans, styles, colours and sizes are well into the millions, a volume of computers were used to do this entirely in a cloud type environment. The ultimate file list generated created the base data and the core of the problem was certainly the fact that certain words both individually and in combination were or became offensive. This was culled from 202,000 words to around 1,100 and ultimately slightly more than 700 were used due to character length and the fact that I wanted to closely reflect the appearance of the original slogan graphically,' added Fowler.

The computer-generated slogans sat on a server until they were indexed by Amazon. The response from customers was immediate disgust. Solid Gold Bomb pulled all computer-generated parody t-shirts from its stores and Amazon channels worldwide. Increasingly, pre-defined algorithms are driving how we engage with content. It's commonplace for a media or ecommerce website to present content based on your viewing habits. Inevitably, sometimes computers make the wrong call and we'd argue that human input is critical both in instances of search and the editorial process.

Motivation: online versus offline

When the Internet makes it so easy to spotlight bad service and organise groups against a common purpose, why isn't brand anarchy or vandalism more commonplace? It's an issue that we returned to time and time again when we were researching this book. In an effort to find some answers I headed online and asked people in my social networks for their views. There can be no doubt that organisations fear the reputational impact of an online attack on their brands and are investing in modernising their communications. These changes will impact every area of an organisation in time as social forms of media force organisations to engage with their customers and staff in a two-way relationship.

'I can't decide if it is because as practitioners we overvalue reputation, if it is because grassroots campaigners, union leaders and non-government organisations (NGOs) haven't yet seen the value in online actions, but in reality, online threats don't affect most businesses in a meaningful way. They are still planning marches, strikes and boycotts,' said Dan Howe, an online marketer for animal-welfare organisation People for the Ethical Treatment of Animals (PETA). There are many exceptional stories of groups that have used the Internet as a medium for change. We've shared many of these stories in *Brand Vandals*. But these are the exception rather than the norm.

Then there's the issue of access and literacy. 'We've still a long way to go to the point where everyone is literate online and happy to share their views. There are still huge swathes of people who don't have access to a computer, let alone broadband,' said Sarah Hall, managing director of Sarah Hall Consulting, a public relations consultancy based in the North East of England and a board member of the CIPR in the UK.

'Everything's easy when you know how, but it's still a minority of people across privileged demographics that have the know-how and they're going to stay apathetic while life is good,' said Joy Stefanicki.

Stefanicki is a founder of SxSE London, a grassroots social and digital media festival that brings together activists in their respected industries, using social and digital media to implement change. Her point is well made. Access to the Internet has made it too easy to share our opinions and form groups. The cost of engagement is 140 characters and a hashtag on Twitter. On Facebook or Google+ all that's required is a click to add your support to a cause. It's as close to effortless as is possible, whereas motivating a group to take direct action offline in a meaningful way takes work.

'The big social movements such as the Arab Springs are outliers, not the norm. To achieve scale in search rankings requires a catalyst – a television appearance or a celebrity, for example. Those are undemocratic catalysts. There needs to be a movement or movements to help common purposes take shape and rise more quickly up the rankings. There is now an easy way for people to express in words and images online, but there is no easy way for people to accelerate this offline,' added Mark Adams, chairman, the Conversation Group, a global social media consultancy.

Each of the issues raised remains a work in progress. Digital access and literacy is improving, NGOs are getting smarter in their use of technology and new organisations such as 38 Degrees are tackling the issue of offline empowerment. Two billion people are set to join the Internet in the next decade and organisations have no choice but to embrace social forms of media as a means of engagement with staff and customers. Our view is that we're at the very beginning of what is possible and that brand vandalism will become a way of life for citizens and organisations in the future.

CHAPTER 3

HOW BAD COULD IT GET?

Who are the individuals that are holding organisations to account and how are they doing it? #BrandVandals

Customer service and customer relationship management are the next frontier in social engagement between an organisation and its audiences. Brands are spending huge amounts of money creating content and building communities to engage prospective customers in a participative relationship. It's working. Consumers are highly engaged with the biggest brands via Facebook, Twitter and owned media properties. Consumers want to use these nascent channels to engage with organisations. The lifecycle of a branded Twitter account will typically see it discovered by consumers and used as a customer service channel within a matter of weeks. Brands will persist in building their network and sharing editorial content in a bid to engage with their audience and either ignore criticism or redirect it to traditional customer service channels.

Tweet washing: Marks & Spencer

When Howard Walker pre-ordered Christmas dinner for his family from Marks & Spencer (M&S) he didn't expect to have to queue in store for 45 minutes on Christmas Eve. He didn't expect to be told by a shop assistant that online orders are tricky and he didn't expect to have to surrender his trolley to an M&S trolley collector as he left the store and lug £200 worth of shopping to his car. But this is exactly what happened after he placed an order via the Internet to collect from the Newcastle store. The trolley incident was the final straw but it neatly encapsulates the futility of this situation. Walker lost his token when he forcibly had to give up his trolley. M&S would later send him a trolley token to replace the one he'd surrendered. You might call it the ultimate token gesture.

Walker's story shows up the gap between the narrative that brands are creating online thanks to the social web versus the reality of the silos that exist in large organisations. Corporate structures are defined along operational functions. Communications and reputation management, traditionally the domain of public relations, is distinct from marketing, sales and customer service. The social web is showing up these organisational silos and forcing greater levels of integration and flatter structures.

Walker turned to Twitter to air his frustration. It's a form of brand vandalism that is increasingly used by consumers when a product or service provided by an organisation fails to meet their expectation. It has no respect for traditional customer service channels. After all, it's much easier to send a 140-character message than to complete an online form or navigate a complex telephone call centre to speak to an overseas operator. Savvy communications teams at organisations such as M&S have invested in monitoring to spot online grumbles from customers, such as Walker, although in this instance it wasn't necessary as he directed his tweet to M&S directly. There then followed an exchange of messages that concluded with Howard being directed to a form on the M&S webpage to submit a complaint. Christmas came and went and the incident was forgotten until the New Year.

In the first week of January Walker retold the story via a note posted to the M&S customer service webpage. He received a response, quickly, thanking him for his email and apologising for the incident. That would have been an end to the saga but for two paragraphs at the end of the email that stated that the email was sent from an account that didn't accept responses and that if he wished to respond he'd need to head back to the website. M&S is clearly investing a significant amount in engaging with customers via Twitter but at the first sign of brand vandalism it is shifting the conversation off the social network and back to its traditional customer services channels. This is because of the silo that exists between communications and customer service. Walker called this Tweet-washing[17].

It's a very typical response from a brand. I may be @wadds on Twitter but I doubt that's a moniker that exists on any customer relationship management database for an organisation where I'm a customer. Change is coming but we're at a point in time when organisations are frequently overwhelmed by customer engagement via new channels such as Twitter and simply aren't able to reengineer processes or technology fast enough. This wasn't the end of Walker's story. He shared his blog post with his network via Twitter and it received a significant number of retweets and in an ironic turn of events prompted M&S to ask him to send a private message via Twitter with his email address so that the issue could be explored further.

Media change in Northumberland

Public sector organisations are frequently criticised for being being slow to innovate and get to grips with media change. Not so Northumberland County Council. Ross Wigham[18] has seen the changes in the media and organisational communications first hand. He trained as a journalist at the turn of the century and spent five years working in editorial roles for a variety of Reed Business publications before applying his skills as a corporate communicator in the public sector. A period as a media relations manager for Gateshead Council was followed by a

---

17 Howard Walker. 'Tweet-washing: a 21st century retail breakdown, Version One.' http://howardwal.wordpress.com/2013/01/13/tweetwashing/ (13, January 2013)
18 Ross Wigham. http://adaywithoutoj.com

seemingly meteoric rise to head of communications at Northumberland County Council. But, as we're to discover, it was with good reason.

Northumberland is an unusual place. I have a huge affection for the county as it's been my family's home for the last five years. It is the largest but least populated county in England. It has 300,000 inhabitants spread over 2,000 square miles. A lot of its citizens are located in remote locations. It's also a financially diverse community. Areas of relative poverty sit alongside prosperity. The economy in Northumberland was once made up of coal mining, agriculture and large feudal estates. Coal mining is long gone, replaced to relatively small degree by rural businesses, retail and tourism. Many of the estates have been broken up but some remain as significant business concerns, most notably Northumberland Estates, overseen by Ralph Percy the 12th Duke of Northumberland. There is a small, but growing community of professionals such as myself who work from home, or travel to Newcastle, Edinburgh, London or further afield for work.

Northumberland County Council was formed in 2009 following the structural changes to local government in the UK. In a process of rationalisation unitary authorities were created in parts of the country which had previously operated a two-tier system of counties and districts. In Northumberland this meant that the local councils in Alnwick, Berwick, Blyth, Morpeth, Tynedale and Wansbeck were merged to create the 1,800-person county council with a £800 million budget headquartered in Morpeth. It was a significant undertaking by any measure.

Wigham and I met over a cup of tea at his office at County Hall in Morpeth. It's everything you'd expect of a 1960s local government building made up of a rabbit warren of corridors and offices. But Wigham is quick to overcome my prejudices of a public sector bureaucrat. He says that he was initially suspicious of social, or vanity media, as he labelled it, following conferences and events that he attended in the late noughties. Northumberland County Council's initial response was to create a Facebook page that mirrored news updates from its website but that the efforts of the communications team were mainly focused on media relations and a print newsletter. Their attitude changed in December 2009 when Northumberland faced a hard winter. Heavy falls of snow shut roads and schools for more than two weeks in the run-up to Christmas. The council turned to Facebook to post updates about closures. There were lots. 'Facebook allowed us to communicate clearly each morning which schools would be open and which roads were closed,' said Wigham.

Dealing with brand vandals

Wigham is candid about the council's early efforts. 'A council's default position with the local media is typically suspicion and tension. We assumed that this would be the same when it came to engaging with social media. My team spent weeks developing process and content plans to deal with worse case scenarios. I honestly don't think we've looked at them since. We've found that the public are a lot more reasonable than journalists,' he said.

It's an interesting point. Wigham says that it's typical for a member of the Facebook community to respond to a query on the Facebook page before a member of the communications team has had a chance to engage. But surely there must have been instances of brand vandalism where someone has hijacked Northumberland County Council's channels and posted inappropriate content? Wigham reckons not. Instances of abuse are few and far between he says. 'We've had one situation where an individual with a complaint about a council traffic diversion posted his gripe on every single post on our

Facebook page. It was blatantly spam and we were already addressing the issue directly. In three years it's the only time that we have had to delete content off Facebook. We expected a lot more drama,' he said.

In December 2010 Northumberland faced a second bout of snow. It was more prolonged than the previous year. My children worked remotely using digital learning methods for almost three weeks. The council's, by now well-established, Facebook and Twitter networks sprang into action again as emergency communications channels. This time the dialogue was constant and two-way. The council posted information and schools and citizens responded with local road and weather conditions. People were more than happy to share information, said Wigham, providing intelligence to the council's army of snow ploughs and gritters.

It may have been a series of extreme weather events that convinced Northumberland County Council of the value of social media as a means of direct engagement but it has become a cornerstone of its communications efforts. Wigham says that there are distinct communities and characters on Facebook, Twitter and the website. Facebook is used for ongoing dialogue, Twitter for campaigns and the website as an information repository.

Building direct relationships

In the four months prior to our meeting Wigham says that the council has engaged directly with at least 10 per cent of its potential audience. When I follow up with him after our meeting I ask him to justify this figure. He digs out the numbers directly from analytic reports: 9,736 people have interacted with the council on Facebook and there have been 8,706 mentions or retweets on Twitter. In the last 12 months the council has curated content around the Olympics and a royal visit. It has promoted residents' weekends using social media and has continued to use the social channels that it has developed for day-to-day citizen engagement. The communications team explores new forms of social media as they emerge. It has developed more than 60 Pinterest boards for different attractions, locations and events in the county pulling together almost 2,000 pieces of content.

'Social media has enabled us to build direct relations and demonstrate the work of the council,' says Wigham. Where the council has led, others have followed. Local media and tourism organisations have been quick to engage with its work, joining in conversations via hashtags and curating content. Wigham's department has become a magnet for students who want to gain work experience and understand how social media is used to engage with citizens in the public sector. It's no surprise that Wigham and his colleagues have won awards for their work.

Fortnum & Mason unmoved by PETA anti-foie gras campaign

Some of the most innovative yet under-reported public relations work is delivered by the third sector. Budgets are tight for charity and campaign groups but there is more opportunity to take risk than in the public or private sector. I caught up with Dan Howe, online marketer for animal-welfare organisation People for the Ethical Treatment of Animals (PETA). We met in Drink, Shop & Do, a retro design shop and café bar around the corner from his office in Caledonian Road. It's an upcoming part of London thanks to the redevelopment of Kings Cross and St Pancras. Howe was reflecting on a campaign by PETA to force upmarket retailer Fortnum & Mason in Piccadilly, London, to stop selling foie gras. It reportedly accounts for two per cent of total sales of foie gras in the UK.

Foie gras is goose liver that is produced by force feeding the animals in what PETA and many people commonly believe to be an inhumane process. Its production is banned in the UK but not its sale. PETA's campaign has generated blanket national press coverage and mobilised a sizable army of advocates across various social media platforms, most notably on Fortnum & Mason's own Facebook page. But the retailer, favoured by the royal family, has held its ground and refuses to be 'bullied' and for now foie gras remains on the shelves.

Fortnum & Mason's CEO Ewan Venters was Selfridge's executive director for food, restaurants and online when it rescinded to PETA's demands to stop stocking foie gras in 2009. He reportedly said that it had been a collective decision taken by the board. PETA produced a short undercover video film of footage, narrated by Sir Roger Moore, showing geese being force fed on farms that allegedly supply Georges Bruck, Fortnum & Mason's supplier.

Fortnum & Mason denies that the farms shown supply it with foie gras. PETA countered this claim, by matching video footage with a farm that appears in Fortnum & Mason's own promotional footage. PETA used its existing contacts to help mobilise the campaign. In the UK it identifies its activists from a database of hundreds of thousands of supporters. Email communications were used to prime activists to lobby via Fortnum & Mason's Facebook, FourSquare, Google Reviews and Twitter profiles. Supporters were also asked to take direct action and email CEO Ewan Venters and Fortnum & Mason's private equity backer Wittington Investments.

'The campaign was launched at midnight on a Saturday night using emails to activists and coordinated support from celebrity influencers, ahead of an exclusive breaking in the *Observer*,' said Howe. YouTube was used as the hosting and sharing platform for the video content. This meant that views and conversations could be collated in a single place and weren't fragmented across other platforms. Timing to provide an element of surprise is critical for success for brand activists such as Howe. He continues to post content after office hours when supporters are online, but public relations teams may not be, so that content has a longer life.

The PETA team seeded the video by using its existing network and contacted celebrity supporters to encourage tweets of support, thus broadening its reach. When the national media were alerted on Monday the video had already had several thousand views. PETA's press office team secured coverage in national newspapers, from the *Mail Online* to the *Telegraph*, and kept media interested by coming up with new angles, such as involving the RSPCA and soliciting opinion articles from industry experts and celebrities.

Trade press in the marketing and retail sectors was also targeted. And with the help of donors, ads were secured in London's commuter papers, which prompted a noticeable spike in online interest and discussion. On Facebook, PETA's 40,000 supporters have all been hit several times over according to analytics for its page. At the beginning of the campaign it paid for modest promoted posts to reach friends of supporters. This, says Howe, provides a cost-effective way to reach a bigger audience that are likely to warm to the campaign. 'Facebook content that generates sympathy or outrage is the most effective way to promote sharing, and with undercover footage of suffering animals, such emotions are easy to generate.'

Fortnum & Mason's own Facebook page is moderated but comments aren't deleted unless they are offensive. It has responded to vandalism from PETA supporters by increasing the frequency of its posts in a bid to bury negative comments. PETA supporters also targeted Google + Reviews. These appear above the fold of a Google search and on Google + Local pages and are seldom monitored by brand owners. On Twitter Howe used pre-loaded tweets directly targeting Fortnum & Mason and its CEO, Ewan Venters. He followed all of its followers and direct messaged anyone who followed back with details of the campaign.

'The hope was that by reaching people that Ewan Venters is influenced by or respects we'd have more sway in convincing him. Targeting and recruiting influential people in niches important to Fortnum & Mason was important early on in the campaign,' said Howe.

The campaign has generated millions of impressions; the video has been viewed over 16,000 times and has undoubtedly caused a few headaches or sleepless nights for Fortnum & Mason's PR, social media and customer service teams. There can be no doubt that the PETA campaign has created a great deal of awareness but it has failed to meet its objective. Howe refuses to answer whether he's accepting a stalemate in the campaign against Fortnum & Mason. His unwillingness to be drawn suggests not.

Calling a council to account on school dinners

Only the most hardened cynic could fail to be inspired by the story of a nine-year-old girl who shamed a Scottish council using a blog, notched up 4.5 million hits, and raised a considerable sum of money for charity. Martha Payne's story started in April 2012 when, as a pupil at Lochgilphead Primary, Argyll, Scotland, she started a blog about her school dinners called NeverSeconds. Martha published photos of her lunches and ranked them for taste, portion size, health and price. Guess what? Martha's reviews weren't always positive. Within a month a community gathered around the blog.

School children and parents from around the world shared photos and information about their own lunches, some of which Martha shared. Dozens of people engaged with the blog via comments on each post. Martha set up a JustGiving account for Mary's Meals, a charity that sets up school feeding projects in some of the world's poorest communities, and invited anyone inspired by her blog to make a donation. In a media savvy move chef Nick Nairn invited Martha along with council and government officials to his cookery school in Stirling to discuss school dinners and cook up some lunches of their own. The resulting write-up in the *Daily Record* under the headline 'Time to fire the dinner ladies...' didn't impress Argyll and Bute Council and it took action via the head teacher at Lochgilphead Primary school, banning Martha from taking photos of her lunch.

But by now the community around NeverSeconds was huge and included the national media. The cocktail of campaigning, censorship, injustice and social media was just too juicy for news desks to ignore. Stories in the national and international media the following morning forced a defensive response from Argyll and Bute Council claiming that the article in the *Daily Record* had, 'led catering staff to fear for their jobs,' and that the NeverSeconds blog, 'misrepresented the options and choices available to pupils'. Three hours later the council backed down. In an updated statement it said that censorship was inappropriate and invited Martha and her father to meet with council officials to discuss school meals.

Martha's blog lives on and the community she has created has donated more than £60,000 to Mary's Meals. It would be very easy to criticise Argyll and Bute Council for handling this situation in such a heavy-handed way but it is no different from any organisation that has failed to recognise that it doesn't own its reputation. In a council's case its reputation lies in the hands of its citizens such as Martha.

It also failed to realise that, thanks to social media, a nine year old can share her opinions with an international audience via the Internet and build a community that, in this instance, caught the attention of campaigners, chefs, politicians and the mainstream media. Whether the quality of school dinners at Lochgilphead Primary will improve we'll only learn by continuing to follow Martha's NeverSeconds blog.

Corporations are people: British Airways

In November 2012 the Twitter account for British Airways retweeted a racist and obscene tweet from a customer. The tweet reportedly remained on the airline's Twitter page for up to an hour. The first that most followers of the @british_airways account knew was an apologetic follow-up tweet. The retweet by British Airways was clearly a mistake. I'm speculating, but it's likely, that someone in the customer service team hit 'retweet' on an online management system rather than creating a task or some other element of workflow.

Inevitably, both Twitter users and traditional media outlets criticised British Airways for the error. The response by the airline was spot on, to a point. It deleted the tweet as soon as the error was identified, apologised to its followers and said that it was investigating what may have happened. Here's the issue. Corporations are people. As they become increasingly social, as customers demand, mistakes such as an occasional inappropriate retweet are inevitable.

It is critical that anyone that manages a Twitter account on behalf of an organisation is trained in the rudiments of media law and that robust processes are in place. Even then, errors will occasionally occur. The real story here should be the abuse that corporate Twitter accounts receive from customers. It's not very social is it?

Brands can laugh, too

Brands are becoming more human in the way that they commu-nicate because consumers expect it and those that do earn attention. A sense of humour on the social web can go a long way to diffusing a situation and getting positive attention for your brand. This is the approach that Bodyform, the feminine towel brand, took when Richard Neill posted a tongue-in-cheek rant about the brand's advertising on its Facebook page. 'Hi, as a man I must ask why you have lied to us for all these years. As a child I watched your advertisements with interest as to how at this wonderful time of the month the female gets to enjoy so many things. I felt a little jealous. I mean, bike riding, roller-coasters, dancing, parachuting, why couldn't I get to enjoy this time of joy and "blue water" and wings.'

Neill claims that Bodyform's advertising misled him into believing that women using its products engage in all sorts of physical activity during their period. He says that he felt conned when he got a girlfriend and discovered that this wasn't the case. The post got more than 10,000 likes and 4,500 comments and was reported as a flippant story by the mainstream media. Bodyform responded with a two-minute video posted on YouTube of a fictional CEO, Carolyn Williams, played by an actress.

'Hi Richard. We loved your post on our Facebook page. We are always grateful for input from our users, but your comment was particularly poignant. If Facebook had a "love" button, we'd have clicked it. But it doesn't. So we've made you a video instead. Unfortunately Bodyform doesn't have a CEO. But if it did she'd be called Caroline Williams. And she'd say this.'

In the video Williams apologises and admits that Bodyform has lied in its advertisements. She says that the advertisements aren't a factual representation of events and are in fact meta-phors used to protect men from the reality of periods. During the six weeks after the video was posted it was viewed almost 3.5 million times and generated thousands of comments on Facebook and YouTube.

Some brands don't use a sense of humour as part of their corporate tone of voice to engage with their customers in this way. Holiday firm Thomas Cook missed an opportunity when an individual called Thomas Cook posted a cheeky message on its UK Facebook page. 'Seeing as I share the exact same name as your huge company, and because of this I have been ridiculed for as long as I can remember, I think it's only fair that you help compensate for this by giving me one of your lovely holidays.'

The company has a good engagement and content strategy on Facebook and is typically quick to deal with customer complaints and move them off the page to a direct one-to-one channel. That is exactly what happened in this situation but despite encouragement from other Thomas Cook followers to spotlight the potential public relations opportunity, the company responded with a dry message saying that unfortunately it was unable to give away holidays and asking Cook to visit the company's website for the best available prices.

The story doesn't end there. Cook gave Thomas Cook a second chance, explaining, clearly tongue-in-cheek, that he wasn't look for a free holiday but compensation for years of ridicule for sharing the same name as the holiday company. He suggested that a weekend in Paris would suffice. Meanwhile Thomas Cook competitor, lowcostholidays.com, spotted a social marketing opportunity and contacted Cook by direct message via Facebook offering him a holiday. 'Here at lowcostholidays. com we completely sympathise with your suffering and if your name was "lowcostholidays.com", we would certainly have accepted your request to be sent away on a weekend in Paris. So how about we send you on that weekend in Paris?'

Cook took the trip and uploaded a photo from Paris to his

Facebook account, which was shared widely both on Facebook and Twitter. Like Bodyform the newspaper and television journalists spotted a great story and news of Cook's lowcostholidays. com trip to Paris was reported widely, generating mainstream media attention for the competitor. Savvy communicators can turn acts of brand vandalism into opportunities.

#WaitroseReasons Twitter gaffe

Sometimes efforts by brands to engage with customers can simply go wrong and unless a brand has a crisis plan in place and is quick to react, sustained reputational damage can result. Consumers may simply not respond as you expect when you ask them to engage with your brand. The best laid plans can backfire and when they do the social media failure can become a story in its own right.

In September 2012 Waitrose, the upmarket UK supermarket, invited customers to complete the tweet 'I shop at Waitrose because...' and sign-off with the hashtag #WaitroseReasons. The request was too much for Twitter users who took the opportunity to poke fun at Waitrose and its reputation for being a destination for upmarket shoppers. Here are some example tweets.

I shop at Waitrose because Tesco doesn't stock Unicorn food #waitrosereasons

I shop at #Waitrose because I WILL NOT stand next to the scumbags at Marks and Spencer. #waitrosereasons

I shop @waitrose because their swan burgers are good enough for the queen #waitrosereasons

I shop at Waitrose so people know I'm filthy rich and therefore automatically better than they are #waitrosereasons

The campaign lit up Twitter and went viral but not for the reasons that Waitrose expected. Waitrose responded in good humour, tweeting 'Thanks for all the genuine and funny #WaitroseReasons tweets. We always like to hear what you think and enjoyed reading most of them.'

Consumers are typically forgiving of an honest and humorous answer and it is unlikely that the incident did Waitrose any harm. In fact it could have been brave and gone further rewarding the funniest tweets.

The lesson is clear. Never underestimate your customers and plan for when they don't respond as you're hoping.

CHAPTER 4

PIGS AND LIPSTICK

There is nowhere to hide for businesses that are anything less than transparent internally or externally. #BrandVandals

You can't put lipstick on a pig although that's the approach that many organisations take to communications. Reality on the face of it for many organisations looks a lot like a pig. Communications is called upon to apply the make-up in a bid to make organisations look more attractive. Change is coming but it is slow. We have been on a slow evolution to greater levels of transparency in government, society and commerce since World War II. Technology has been a factor in accelerating this change but it isn't the root cause. A shift to a greater level of transparency started occurring long before the invention of the Internet.

'Society has become more transparent during the past six or seven decades. Much has been written about World War II being a class leveller as officers and privates worked closely together in a way never before seen. Certainly the root to a more transparent society lay in the war but if anything it was the postwar consensus that followed in the late 1940s and 1950s that kickstarted the erosion of corporate and societal opacity,' said Andrew Thomas, publishing editor, of *Communicate* magazine.

We first met Thomas in Chapter 2 when he shared his views about non-government organisations that engage in brand vandalism as a means of direct action. He tells a story of cultural and corporate change through the second half of the twentieth century.

'The democratisation of education and the increase of working-class undergraduates brought about change during the 1960s – an academic transparency that continued with the introduction of the Open University. Culturally, the punk explosion in the 1970s instigated a questioning of authority in a way that the revolutionaries of today solely attribute to their social media platforms. This move to greater transparency continued in the 1980s as Prime Minister Margaret Thatcher brought about a number of corporate transparency initiatives to protect a nation of wannabe capitalists in a programme of privatisation,' said Thomas.

Successive generations, ours included, like to claim responsibility for being the catalyst to radical change in society. But history informs us that change is slow and can take generations, even when it results from a revolution or a war.

'If social media has been the finishing line in a race to greater transparency, the final hundred metres must be defined by the many policies introduced by the Blair government. The Freedom of Information Act preceded Wikileaks; transparency initiatives in the extractive industries came before the creation of Facebook and so on,' says Thomas.

We haven't suddenly arrived in a place where society has mobilised a campaign for change using social forms of media. In fact, the social media revolution isn't a revolution at all. Thomas makes a compelling case that the shift to greater levels of organisational transparency results from developments since the 1950s. Changes in society and the legislative framework in the West have coincided with the rise of social media to empower citizens. The result is that we've arrived at a place where transparency is now expected as the norm by individuals, corporations and governments.

Transparency and trust

Kate Bosomworth is the managing director of London-based public relations agency Speed Communications. She works with sports and nutrition brands, helping them to build relationships with consumer audiences via social and traditional media. She has observed changes in consumer behaviour at first hand over the last 10 years and advises clients on how best to respond.

'A gym chain I worked with a few years ago was surprised to see that its members were signing up to train as instructors through its in-house training school. This was designed to train new staff to its high standards, but members were almost equal in numbers. Not because they wanted to change careers, they just wanted to know more about their training, do it better, whether they had an instructor or not. Clever brands are making the most of this thirst for information, expertise and knowledge. The name and picture of the farmer who grew the potatoes in Yorkshire that made your bag of sea salt and vinegar crisps is enough to tell you that. A far cry from the plain white bag of Tudor crisps I grew up with. We now expect and demand a connection with the brand in this way – it helps create trust,' said Bosomworth.

Why do we need to trust brands so much more now than we did historically? Because we are more cynical. We don't trust the brands that choose only to broadcast, we are less trusting of claims. We are fuelled by media hype and, sadly, an ongoing series of damaging scandals that have affected sectors from food, energy, health products – the list goes on. Transparency is all. Consumers have chosen to educate themselves about a whole host of factors that now affect their consumption and buying habits. Why? Because they can. The information is there for the taking and information is empowering – it provides choice.

'If you aren't transparent, consumers will wonder why. Two paths emerge at this point: the path for those who will switch off and go and find a brand that will engage and allow them to participate or the path that leads them to find out their own information, which may or may not be correct. There are millions of opinions and voices online sharing their views, whether they are wrong or right. So, in order to overcome the latter – the point at which the brand loses control – these brands which traditionally may not have been open or shared the information behind their product development, why it works, why it is safe, why it is better, have started to understand that they must,' said Bossomworth.

Rachel Miller is an internal communications and social media strategist who learned her trade as head of communications at London Overground Rail Operations, the organisation responsible for running the London Overground network under a Concession Agreement with Transport for London (TfL). Miller is a smart thinker and doer named by Econsultancy as a Top UK female blogger in 2012 and was listed in *PRWeek*'s Top 29 under 29 professional communicators in 2009.

'Today, transparency is essential and expected by employees, the media, shareholders, customers and future employees alike. Credible communication is key and transparency plays an essential role. Strong communication is authentic; warts and all. It has to include good and bad feedback – if you keep negative comments from employees, you do everyone a disservice to censor them. It's getting harder to hide because the sources of information have broadened,' said Miller.

It's a point with which Thomas wholly agrees. More channels of communication mean that there are fewer places to hide for an errant organisation but he sounds a note of caution, saying that we're a long way from a corporate utopia.

'In the cases where corporate opacity exists for duplicitous reasons then this will not stop. It has always been possible for dodgy companies to be secretive, and when they want to they will continue. It may become harder, and if companies are going to be found out they may be found out sooner, but there will always be corporate scandals such as Barclays with its Libor fixing or Trafigura and its toxic waste dumping. My belief, however, is that corporate criminality is not a recessive trait – the main reason for a lack of transparency is incompetence, and the incompetent CEO will normally be rumbled. Exposure will come from staff, investors, regulators, media and so on. If an organisation is not totally open then these stakeholders are prepared to bring it down,' said Thomas.

Reasons to remain tight-lipped

Radical transparency as proponents of social media demand isn't always possible. There will always be situations that demand a measured, controlled approach with a tight rein on messaging, which mean complete transparency is not always possible. There will always be reasons why companies have to play their cards close to their chests when it comes to company information and communications, but it's usually for good reason, in a set timescale and for a defined purpose. Miller cites the example of corporate finance, merger and acquisition activity or organisation change.

'An example is sensitivities around transformational change, particularly when it involves job losses or radical restructures. A company has to talk with many parties and perhaps union officials, too, so a timed flow of information is critical to ensure the right people are having the right conversations at the right time. This may mean only a small group of impacted employees know what is happening before you're able to share with the whole organisation. This is justifiable because consultation periods allow for plans to be influenced and changed. Communicating accurately is the key,' said Miller.

Legislative issues related to financial disclosure, privacy or security, increasingly drive the corporate communications agenda for government or public sector organisations and publicly quoted companies. It is typically a requirement of a financial market such as the New York or London Stock Exchanges that a publicly traded company discloses any information that is likely to be price sensitive. The typical guiding principal is whether information is likely to cause a share price fluctuation of 10 per cent or more. This could include a change of management, the loss of a key client or a substantive change to business operations. Increasingly this can cover reputational issues where the requirement can be less clear cut.

'If a company is breaking the law, such as dumping toxic waste or breaking local employment regulations, the potential of discovery, and subsequent financial penalties, obviously require disclosure. But what if a company followed legislation, but not best practice? There is a history of what is best practice today becoming enshrined in legislation tomorrow. What if it is a business practice that can be attacked by pressure groups? What can be described as 'price sensitive' is an incredibly grey area,' said Thomas.

The reality is that corporate misbehaviour is likely to be spotlighted by consumers through social media channels if an organisation tries to filter, spin or withhold information. Organisations need to be on the front foot in communicating with their audiences and proactively manage their reputation.

Communications matters of life and death

In the health sector it is much more difficult. Here, organisational communications can literally be a matter of life and death. Sarah Pinch was the communications director of University Hospitals Bristol NHS Foundation Trust for nearly five years before starting her own company, Pinch Point Communications. She's a board member of the CIPR in the UK, and in 2011 was the winner of the CIPR and the Institute of Directors' Public Relations Director of the Year award.

Pinch cites the Caldicott guidelines that prevent information for patients who are treated by the NHS in England and Wales from being shared[19]. It arose as the result of a review commissioned in 1997 by the chief medical officer of England, owing to increasing concern about the ways in which patient information was being used and the need to ensure that confidentiality was not undermined. The primary driver was the development and use of information technology in the service, and its capacity to disseminate information about patients rapidly and extensively.

'The NHS, under the Caldicott guidelines, has very serious rules about who can access patient information. If the media asks for information about a patient, the NHS cannot give it without the patient's permission. It can be hugely challenging to explain this to journalists, especially if someone has already put some information into the public domain. It makes communications with the media challenging and, at times, very difficult. It can look like the NHS is purposefully withholding information to make itself look better, when it is only ever doing so because of patient confidentiality,' said Pinch.

Communicating complex issues is another challenge for organisations. Sometimes simplifying information leads to misunderstanding. In the public sector the drive to benchmark organisations has led to a league table mentality that presents data without any context. It's an issue that frequently arises in the medical field. If you're comparing the performance of two doctors with different levels of experience working on different caseloads then simply comparing outcomes can lead to the wrong answer. Facts and figures can suddenly become hugely emotive.

19 *The Caldicott Report*. Oxford Radcliffe Hospitals NHS Trust, http://confidential.oxfordradcliffe.net/caldicott/report/ (April 2003)

'If Doctor A is one of the most highly experienced heart surgeons, she is enormously respected by her colleagues, her royal college; she is an internationally renowned lecturer and trainer for other surgeons and because of her experience and knowledge she operates on some of the sickest, most complex cases, then the chances are more of her patients will die, than Doctor B, who is a relatively new surgeon and operates on some of the most straightforward cases and more of his patients live. Does that mean Doctor A is a worse doctor? Because the statistics say more of her patients die?' asked Pinch.

Yes disclosure of information is important but framing data with context is critical as Pinch makes plainly clear.

Everyone is a spokesperson: employee role

Brand Vandals aren't just members of your external audience. Sometimes they can be employees. A lack of robust processes in an organisation can lead to mishaps and internal bouts of brand vandalism. As journalists at the outset of our careers on local and trade papers, we made a virtue of this fact and would occasionally get tip-offs from employees or their relatives about news from an employer. It typically occurred when the news was negative and concerned layoffs, pay freezes or trade union disputes, and an organisation was making attempts to cover it up. Our response was to call up the organisation concerned and ask the receptionist leading questions such as, 'I'm calling to speak to human resources about the redundancies that you're making.' It was very easy to stand up most stories in this way. It's not a particularly ethical tactic and I'm not proud of it, but it almost always worked.

Now employees communicate freely online and everyone is a spokesperson irrespective of whether they mark up their social media profiles with a note about personal disclosure. It's an issue that is frequently catching organisations out, according to *Communicate* magazine's Thomas.

'People don't seem to realise that if there is a quote about a company from an employee then a journalist will use that as an official source. A journalist is very unlikely to source a quote to Twitter as it makes them look lazy but they will most likely source it to the originator of the tweet. And if they don't assign the tweet to a named individual then the person who sent out the tweet is likely to be cited as a company insider...or sources within the company,' said Thomas.

Sourcing a story from social media is a tactic that you see played out in social media every day. The implication for professional communicators is clear: there is no line between personal and professional. Thomas believes that anyone working in communications has to realise that they have no platform, that it is purely personal. If an individual has a profile on social media they are always on duty and always representing their organisation.

Impact on employee communications

Social media has no respect for the traditional hierarchies within an organisation. Connections have always been made across boundaries and departments thanks to information networks such as the smoking corner, the football team or squash club but now internal organisation has been flattened thanks to technologies that allow instant communication and social networks such as Facebook, LinkedIn, Twitter and Yammer.

'Top-down hierarchical command and control-style communication is prevalent in many organisations, however social media is offering a different way of communicating and providing new opportunities for two-way conversations. Employees are being empowered to choose what suits them and to make their own connections with peers and people at all levels of organisations,' said Miller. 'This is hugely exciting because the possibilities for effective internal communications are increasing as organisations realise the potential of equipping employees with the ability to communicate across geographies, functions and grades. This has always happened – cross-departmental chats in the smoking area, for example – but social media has the potential to add a new dynamic to employee relationships.'

As we mentioned in the introduction Steve Earl and I both moved jobs recently and joined large organisations. In the period between our appointments being announced in the trade press and us each starting our new roles, individuals from each organisation made contact with us directly via social networks notably LinkedIn and Twitter. These new introductions and connections occurred spontaneously without the support of the human resources department or management intervention. It meant that on the first day in our new jobs we had already established networks.

It's no surprise, then, that social communication within an organisation is an area where software firms are investing heavily. Firms such as Microsoft are on the acquisition trail for communications platforms and tools such as Yammer. Microsoft has traditionally provided software applications to drive workplace productivity and wants to ensure that it remains relevant to enterprise organisations as they become increasingly social.

Blowing the whistle on organisations

Despite organisations making a huge shift to communication transparency and engagement with employees, we have discovered we are a long way from a nirvana of organisational transparency. Perhaps the best indication is that whistle-blowing remains commonplace. It's a two-way street. Social media makes it easier than ever before for employees to leak information about an organisation's errant behaviour. Miller believes employees will always defy the rules and vent their frustration publically. The challenge for organisations is that social media can quickly amplify information via networks.

'In an ideal world employees will speak with the powers that be in their organisation and not share sensitive or damaging information publicly. However, in reality, there will always be people who choose to flout the rules; usually for effect or because they are unsure what the rules are. People who whistle-blow clearly feel compelled to do so and have their own motivations. Social media simply provides more choice as to how the message is shared and the size of the audience,' said Miller.

Whistle-blowing has always happened in organisations and will continue to do so; it can't be stopped just as an organisation cannot control what people think or say about it, either privately or publicly. Pinch experienced it first hand in her role in the NHS and takes a very pragmatic viewpoint. 'If all the employees of every NHS Trust never made mistakes, never got it wrong, whistle-blowing would never happen; but because of mistakes and learning from them people are living longer and highly premature babies are surviving. Mistakes happen, people die. Learning from those mistakes is what drives improvements and delivers more lifesaving treatments.'

Whistle-blowing then is a fact of life. It is the safety valve of organisational communications. It isn't going to go away as a result of social media. In fact, it's more likely to increase. It can't be stopped and communicators need to deal with it as they deal with other forms of communication. We return to the need for clear communication and transparency. Miller advocates having clear guidance in place for employees, including processes to deal with whistle-blowing and whistle-blowers.

'It is possible to have crystal-clear guidance in place, but in the same way it's possible to have a map of a city in front of you to follow, you can still get lost and make a wrong turn. The key is how you get back on track. Accountability is critical and employees need to know what internal processes and communications exist and what the consequences are. Organisations who think they can ban or stop whistle-blowing are foolhardy. You have to trust employees, reinforce positive behaviour and a culture of openness and coach leaders and people at all levels to listen as well as speak,' said Miller.

One of the best outcomes when whistle-blowing happens is the review of internal processes when a company admits it got things wrong and takes steps to rebuild and openly communicate with employees. It is a healthy means of rebuilding trust. 'Choosing not to review post-situation doesn't work. Your employees will be doing it anyway and have their own opinions about the issues that have been raised. It's far better to be part of and help shape those conversations than pretend they aren't happening,' said Miller.

Driving up standards

So is social media a means to spotlight issues and drive-up standards or a channel for people to air grievances that may or may not be well founded? Miller clearly recognises the juxtaposition of the issue. 'I don't think they are mutually exclusive because social media can be used for both of these things – it can be a way to bring an issue into the limelight, which leads to a drive in standards, and can also be used as a channel for people to air grievances. However, I would hope it is not the only way to communicate issues and grievances. Most of the examples that immediately spring to mind are negative,' said Miller.

Miller cited the example of ailing high street retailer HMV that occurred a few weeks before we spoke in spring 2013. HMV failed to make the transition fast enough from bricks and mortar to online and so lost market share to online stores such as Amazon, disruptive technology such as Apple's iTunes and innovative new Internet services such as Spotify.

The result was that the company went into administration in January 2013 putting 4,500 jobs at risk. During a meeting with the administrator the angry marketing executive used the company Twitter account @hmvtweets to share news of staff redundancies. Seven subversive tweets were posted before HMV regained control of the account and deleted the messages. The lesson from this story and others of its type is that organisations must have robust governance and risk management in place so that when an employee leaves a company the username and password for branded social media accounts aren't left open to abuse. The impact of social media on brands is neatly illustrated by the opportunity for vendors who are helping organisations make sense of the fragmented media environment.

When employees resort to using social media as the outlet for their grievances an organisation clearly has major issues. In HMV's case it was financial ruin. Whether or not employee concerns are well founded there should be structures in place and ways for employees to engage in two-way conversations about their concerns. 'Driving up standards should be part of business as usual. When they are raised as a direct result of issues being highlighted, particularly via social media, it is hard not to feel sceptical about their sincerity. Proactive rather than reactive continuous improvement is critical. Employees should to be encouraged to be honest and give their feedback through appropriate channels and coach leaders to address and respond,' said Miller.

All media is social

For now, social media is feared by most organisations. But if there's one thing we've learned in researching *Brand Vandals* it's that it isn't going to go away. Customers will demand that organisations are social and when they aren't they may go elsewhere. Employees will drive the change and we will see organisations shift from a permissions culture to one of acceptability and inevitably about social tools. Miller reckons that it is going to take around 10 years or so. Mark up 2023 or thereabouts in your diary!

'In the same way we can't imagine working without mobiles, Internet and email, collaborative communications will simply be the way we do business. I doubt it will even have a name within 10 years. I think it will be demystified and standardised and the fear will be reduced. I think language choice has a huge role to play here. We're talking about knowledge sharing, information management, saving time, reducing duplicated effort, connecting employees...all of these skills and competencies are welcomed in organisations. Yet if the way they are achieved is via social forms of communication, fear creeps in,' said Miller.

Miller believes that each organisation needs to develop its own language. The focus should be on the conversations and the actions that are driven from them. 'Many companies are taking tentative steps, whereas some are years into their social communication journeys already. Whatever stage you're at, enjoy it. Listen, learn, evolve and adapt your approach as you go. Your customers and employees will soon let you know when you get it wrong – don't be afraid to make mistakes, as long as you learn from them,' said Miller.

Social media wake-up call for laggards

We're often asked how to convince sceptical managers of the value and benefit of social media. In fact it was a topic that was raised at a recent conference where I gave a keynote speech on social media and reputation management. The digital marketing event in London was hosted by the Association of Colleges[20]. The audience was made up of communications and marketing practitioners from further education colleges in the UK. The primary audience for colleges is 16 to 18 year olds seeking both academic and vocational qualifications. Every piece of available data reports that this audience segment has a voracious appetite for social media and its consumption of traditional media is diminishing fast.

The panel suggested the following as a wake-up call for managers who do not recognise the value of digital communications:

- **Crisis** – a crisis event shines a bright light on communications processes and structures that aren't fit for purpose. Communications need to be transparent and in real time.
- **Monitor** – explore the conversations taking place on forums and social networks about your organisation, location or market. There will almost certainly be a reason that you need to join in.
- **Search** – head to Google and search for your organisation. This is what your customers and prospects will do. How does your organisation perform against its competitors?
- **Influence** – explore online influencers for your location and market. These may be journalists, public officials or business leaders. But they are more likely to be bloggers, or your own customers or prospects.

---

20 *Social media wake-up call for laggards.* Ketchum, http://blog.ketchum.com/social-media-wake-up-call-for-laggards/ (11, December 2011)

- **Traditional media** – look out for the stories that have been written about your organisation online and in traditional media. What's the reaction to stories in the comments? Your organisation should almost certainly be part of these conversations.

Undoubtedly it's a generational issue. There are still managers who have their emails printed out by an assistant and who don't dabble on the Internet unaccompanied. On a recent flight from London to Brussels I sat next to a bureaucrat who was carefully hand writing responses to emails that had been printed out and bound in a neat lever-arch file. But the writing is on the wall and it's likely to be a Facebook wall. Organisations that fail to recognise the changing habits of their audience simply won't be able to reach or engage with them in the future.

CHAPTER 5

THE CLIMATE OF RISK

Citizens have a greater opportunity than ever before to voice opinions, yet levels of disillusionment are higher than ever. What's broken? #BrandVandals

Jaron Lanier is a computer scientist best known for popularising virtual reality. He was one of the Silicon Valley intellectuals that pioneered much of the thinking around the social web in the late 1990s and turn of the millennium. But as social media went mainstream Lanier turned his back on it. In his book *You Are Not a Gadget*[21] he cites the wisdom of the crowd saying that the ability of groups to form online around an issue was more likely to result in online lynch mobs than a move towards greater enlightenment. 'Emphasizing the crowd means de-emphasizing individual humans in the design of society, and when you ask people not to be people, they revert to bad, mob-like behaviours,' he stated.

It's a point well made. The social web provides a populist viewpoint. Content is voted up or down based on votes or shares on Reddit, Mashable and YouTube, and algorithms drive links up and down your Facebook newsfeed depending on the actions of your networks. Even without machine intervention your Google + and Twitter networks self-organise content. Thanks to my social networks my afternoon media diet consists of Google +, Facebook and Twitter. It's dangerous. Content coalesces around a centre of mediocrity driven by algorithms and networks.

Lanier now plies his trade as a scholar at Microsoft research and as a critical voice on the SXSW to TED conference circuit.

---

21 Jaron Lanier. *You Are Not A Gadget: A Manifesto*, Vintage Books (January 2011)

He believes that technology is driving a chasm in society and squeezing the economy. It's not a new viewpoint. As long ago as 2000 he wrote in *Edge* about his unease with technology. 'For the last 20 years, I have found myself on the inside of a revolution, but on the outside of its resplendent dogma. Now that the revolution has not only hit the mainstream, but bludgeoned it into submission by taking over the economy, it's probably time for me to cry out my dissent more loudly than I have before.'

In an interview for *Smithsonian Magazine* in January 2013[22] Lanier cited the development of products such as Google Translate to support his thesis. This product is a free statistical multi-lingual machine translation web service provided by Google to translate from one language to another. Upload text or point it at a webpage in a different language and it will return the result at the click of a button in another language. The artificial intelligence that drives the product makes the result appear almost magical.

But Lanier doesn't mark this down as progress.

'There's another way to look at it,' he told *Smithsonian Magazine*, 'which is the technically true way: you gather a ton of information from real live translators who have translated phrases, just an enormous body of information, and then when your example comes in, you search through that to find similar passages and you create a collage of previous translations.' Lanier claims that technological developments such as this have not contributed to an expansion in wealth but have instead led to an attack on the middle classes. We haven't created an information economy so much as we've made information free and are destroying an economy in the process.

---

22 Ron Rosenbaum. 'What Turned Jaron Lanier Against the Web?' *Smithsonian Magazine*, http://www.smithsonianmag.com/ideas-innovation/What-Turned-Jaron-Lanier-Against-the-Web-183832741.html (January 2013)

'Information doesn't deserve to be free. It is an abstract tool; a useful fantasy, a nothing. It is non-existent until and unless a person experiences it in a useful way,' he said. It's a powerful rhetoric but Lanier saves his greatest ire for the so-called 'drive-by anonymity' as the greatest danger and ultimate threat to the social web. The ability for individuals to hide behind anonymous online monikers isn't liberation for freedom of speech; it's a threat to the fabric of society. When an individual conceals their identity and posts on the Internet they set themselves outside the laws and rules of society. It's a dangerous place.

'Look what we're setting up here in the world today. We have economic fear combined with everybody joined together on these instant twitchy social networks, which are designed to create mass action. What does it sound like to you? It sounds to me like the prequel to potential social catastrophe. I'd rather take the risk of being wrong than not be talking about that.'

Mind your data

Social media enthusiasts happily log their location on social networks such as Facebook and FourSquare via mobile devices. This contributes to an individual's social graph and provides networks with valuable location information. A project at the University of Birmingham showed that it is possible to predict the location of an individual at a point in the future based on data from their mobile phone[23]. The algorithm, developed by Mirco Musolesi, Manlio Domenico, and Antonio Lima, combines location-based tracking with data from the people in your phone book. It won first prize in

---

23 *Interdependence and Predictability of Human Mobility and Social Interactions.* University of Birmingham, http://research.nokia.com/files/public/mdc-final 306_dedomenico.pdf (August 2012)

Nokia's 2012 Mobile Data Challenge to find interesting applications for the interpretation of mobile data.

The research team claims that data from your own phone can be used to predict your location in the next 24 hours to within about a kilometre. Add data from two or three friends and it's possible to get to within 20m. Human beings are social animals and our interaction with friends is predictable. This data is already being captured by mobile phone networks and social networks such as Facebook and FourSquare. It's not much of a stretch of the imagination to envisage how the University of Birmingham project could be used by governments to predict the movement of citizens or by companies wanting to lure mobile phone users with details of shops and restaurants.

Now there's a new game in town that could provide brands with an even deeper level of data. Quantified self or self-tracking is a growing area of the social web whereby individuals log and share variables such as heart rate, weight and exercise on the Internet. Data is typically uploaded by a growing array of devices from heart monitors to bathroom scales. Proponents believe that recording aspects of our personal physiology is a route to improved health and well-being. The condition of our bodies is typically only monitored when we're seriously ill or dying. Most people know their age, their height and their weight and will usually lie about one of these three. We pay greater attention to the performance of our cars.

Kevin Kelly is founder and executive editor of *Wired* magazine. His Quantified Self project encourages its participants to log personal healthcare data such as blood pressure, physical activity, weight and blood pressure[24]. Participants in the project

---

24 Kevin Kelly. *Quantified Self*. http://www.quantifiedself.com (Accessed June 2013)

are inevitably self-motivated and aren't necessarily going to benefit from preventative medical advice but the project provides a window to the future of how healthcare might work. Recording personal health data puts the consumer in control of their healthcare and will inevitably lead to a do-it-yourself healthcare system. In future doctors will prescribe applications not medicine, closing the feedback loop between monitoring and personal action.

The rise of so-called cyberchondria, whereby consumers self-diagnose using the Internet is inevitable but the potential market for self-diagnosis and automatic analysis is huge. The technology already exists. Monitoring devices are getting smaller; smartphones have the functionality to record, monitor and share data and back office monitoring systems could be replicated from other markets. To continue the car simile, manufacturers are already deploying automatic diagnosis systems in the automotive sector in high-end vehicles. The positive benefits of self-tracking in terms of social and personal motivation are plain to see but what are the dangers of spraying personal data about our own physiology around the Internet? I sought out the views of Ged Carroll. We first met Carroll – a digital native, who has grown up with the Internet – in Chapter 2.

'Inevitably, shiny new technologies trigger excitement but I'd caution fans of self-tracking to think through the consequences of organisations harvesting the data that they are publishing,' said Carroll. Health insurance firms place additional premiums on amateur athletes who only train on the weekends or travel to overseas events. A quick check of a Facebook or Twitter account would quickly identify anyone in this category. Likewise, car and house insurance companies base premiums on how frequently your house is left empty and how much you travel. Facebook and FourSquare profiles already provide sufficient data on which to base a calculation. 'Self-tracking adds massive amounts of data to your personal data pool and social graph and raises huge privacy concerns that users need to be cognisant of,' said Carroll.

We should be inherently sceptical, or at least have a degree of scepticism around social networks, cautions Carroll, and be wary of how they may be used in the future. They are free for a reason and that's because the product is your personal data. Google's corporate motto is famously, 'Don't be evil'. Is Google evil? I asked Carroll. His response was typical of the argument often used by technologists to explain the impact of new technologies on humanity. The technology isn't evil; that comes down to its application and how it is used. 'It's like lots of things: opiates aren't evil. They have their use in palliative care, medical pain management and have inspired generations of English literature, from Byron to Burroughs. But if I ever have kids I wouldn't be happy with them using them,' said Carroll.

It's a harsh metaphor but it makes the point.

Carroll spent 13 months working at Yahoo! Europe from 2005. He worked on its search engine, its photo-sharing network, Flickr, and on its bookmarking network, del.icio.us. He describes the open attitude that its engineers had to data formats. Providing the means for customers to export their photos or bookmarks kept the organisation honest; moving to a competitor was just a couple of clicks away and this helped them build great products. The current generation of social networks simply don't have that level of openness. 'Facebook, Google + and Twitter are all effectively closed networks. Yes, there are means to connect other applications so that you can utilise your own data elsewhere but you try exporting your contacts, status updates or photographs. It's inherently difficult to get your data out,' he said.

Here's an irony. As vendors have sought to build tools and monetise the social web it has become increasingly antisocial. Carroll cites Twitter shutting off RSS feeds, which enabled tweets to be displayed across platforms other than Twitter, as a watershed moment. Instead, firms such as Twitter are using data that resides on their platforms to build commercial services. It's a great opportunity for organisations to use data to build profiles for customers. Meanwhile, consumers need to be mindful that whatever data they are sharing with their social networks is likely to be used in some way at some point by an organisation.

There is no such thing as 'free'.

Time to question political engagement

One of my favourite observations from Twitter that demonstrates the gap between political engagement and the apparent apathy for political debate is the Twitter hashtag *#bbcqt* for BBC *Question Time* that fires into life at 10.30 p.m. for an hour each Thursday evening.

The programme, hosted by David Dimbleby, is pitched as a topical debate in which guests from politics and the media answer questions posed by members of the public. It is produced by the BBC and pre-recorded earlier the same evening. Viewers typically tweet throughout the show commenting on questions from the audience and responses from the panel. The debate takes place on the programme among the panellists and the audience but also among the audience on Twitter. And guess what? Often the discussion on Twitter is more interesting than the one on television. Engagement levels are such that the anchor frequently mentions the hashtag during the programme and the hashtag frequently trends on Twitter, indicating that it is one of the most popular topics.

In November 2012 the producers of *Question Time* added a virtual panellist to the weekly line-up. Using the account @bbcextraguest on Twitter the sixth panellist makes comments as the programme is broadcast, reacting to what is going on in the programme and responding to other viewers' tweets.

Meaningful relationships

Is it possible to have a meaningful relationship with a brand? We're pushing our study to the fringes of the social sciences but insofar as brands are increasingly mimicking human relationships in a bid to engage with their audience they need to move beyond the basics of human behaviour. No one is going to get far in a relationship if they shout and harass their audience. Yet this is exactly how brands have marketed their products over the last hundred years.

But when brands adopt human behaviours it is so unusual as to appear extraordinary and even unnerving. In February 2013 followers of the JetBlue and SouthWest Twitter feeds witnessed a far-ranging discussion between the two that covered Guitar hero, hip-hop, scrapbooking and the nature of their relationship. The discussion between the two branded accounts started after someone tweeted their frustration at the names of airlines being abbreviated to acronyms. The two accounts ended up having a conversation more akin to a discussion between two friends over a drink. It was familiar and friendly and not what you'd expect from a pair of corporate Twitter accounts.

Brooke Thomas, a communications specialist at SouthWest told the online community *PR Daily* that exchanging tweets with others simply made work more enjoyable and competition less intense[25]. 'Inevitably people in the same industry share similar passions,' she said. 'It mimics human behaviour and it's what you'd expect from a brand'. Comment about the exchange was polarised between surprise and joy.

Is it possible for a brand to engage directly with its audiences via the social web? One-on-one marketing was an illusion sold to the marketing industry by technology vendors in the 1980s as the benefit of customer relationship management (CRM) systems. The reality is that brands market to audience segments by demographic or variables such as interest or location rather than on an individual basis. Social media may change that dynamic. It makes one-on-one engagement possible. This next story explores my personal relationship with a brand developed over a significant period of time. After a ticket mishap I hoped that a train service might help and support me like an old friend, and it did, but only after I vented my fury via Twitter.

Commuting from Northumberland

Northumberland is a beautiful part of the country but work for communications professionals is thin on the ground. My family's move from London was a life decision. We bought an old farmhouse and smallholding and moved in 2008. I have commuted back and forth to London, or beyond, for work ever since.

My typical routine is to head south on a Monday and back north on a Thursday courtesy of East Coast trains. It's a pleasant journey through Northumberland, Yorkshire and Lincolnshire. Occasionally, if I'm travelling to the US or working in continental Europe I fly from Newcastle airport but

---

25 Southwest and JetBlue exchange words on Twitter, http://www.prdaily. com/Main/Articles/Southwest_and_JetBlue_exchange_words_on_ Twitter_13746.aspx (4 February 2013)

wherever possible I prefer the train line along the UK's east coast. It has the familiarity of an old friend. Most people who live in Northumberland and travel regularly to London feel the same way. It's the main artery linking Berwick, Alnmouth and Newcastle with the capital city.

The line has become even more special to me after I discovered, following my grandfather's death last year, that the English Electric Vulcan, one of the diesel traction engines that he had a hand in designing, ran on the route. The East Coast train service is typically very good. Occasionally there are delays but usually the journey passes without incident. I travel first class so that I can have a meal and work en route. I buy tickets in advance to benefit from the advanced purchase deals. A return ticket costs around £150. Thanks to the online booking service you're able to rebook tickets if your plans change. I estimate that I spend around £4,000 to £5,000 per year with the train operator.

East Coast operates a Customer Reward Scheme. Travellers earn 1.5 points per £1 spent on a first class ticket and 1 point per £1 for a standard class tickets. Nine hundred points can be exchanged for a return first class ticket from Northumberland to London. During a year I collect thousands of points. Reward tickets are ordered online and dispatched by post. Last week I was due to head home using a reward ticket – that was until I mislaid the ticket during the week.

My assistant called the East Coast customer support team with the reference number from my online account in a bid to get a replacement ticket. It was a short call. According to East Coast, tickets cannot be reprinted once they have been printed by a train operator. If you've lost your tickets you have no other option but to purchase new ones. I took to Twitter to try and resolve the issue. Over an 18-month period I have developed a jovial relationship with the @EastCoastUK Twitter team at East

Coast. It has helped me out when there have been delays or I've had a scheduling query. But it's a two-way street. I've jumped to its defence when someone in my network has given it a hard time and I frequently praise excellent service.

Transport operators are a standing target for consumers on Twitter. It's almost too easy to pull out your smartphone and rant in 140 characters when something goes wrong. Log on to Twitter at 8 a.m. on a Monday, or indeed any other weekday, and you'll spot people noisily moaning about late trains, filthy trains, overcrowded trains and expensive trains. The fact is that it's much easier to rant with a tweet than to pick up the phone and navigate a telephone tree to be directed to a call centre and eventually speak with a human being. There is also a cathartic quality to angry tweets and they often get a prompt response, whereas other channels fail, because of the reputational implications.

My relationship with @EastCoastUK turned sour. Like the customer service line it said that even though I had an audit trail on my account it was unable to reprint tickets and that I'd have to buy a new ticket. Several people spotted the Twitter conversation and shared my frustration. Others were critical and said that it was my fault that I'd lost the ticket. I readily recognised that this situation is of my own making and that I was at fault. But I hoped that my loyalty to East Coast over the last four years or so and the relationship that I'd built with the brand via Twitter counted for something.

I asked the @EastCoastUK to call me by phone to explain the situation. I had a great conversation with Hannah in the Twitter team who said that she felt really bad about my problem. 'It happens all the time,' she explained. 'I'm really sorry but I don't have any discretion for this sort of situation. You need to speak to the customer service team. I enjoy our tweets,' she said as a parting shot. So do I, to be fair. The

@EastCoastUK Twitter team does a great job. Its challenge, and opportunity, is that it needs to be integrated directly with the customer service function.

I reported my call with Hannah to my Twitter feed.

Next, an email from Alex Singleton, an ex-broadsheet hack in the UK turned heavyweight corporate communicator, popped into my inbox. He'd spotted my tweets and emailed Karen Boswell, managing director of East Coast, copying me in. Singleton doesn't hold back when he spots a story. He'd voluntarily joined my cause. 'I was disappointed and surprised to read on Twitter today about the treatment of Stephen Waddington, who apparently commutes weekly on your rail service between [the North East] and London. I am writing a blog post on your handling of the matter, which strikes me as damaging to your brand and an example of shabby treatment,' said Singleton.

I 'replied all' to Singleton's email and asked Boswell if we could discuss my situation by phone. I also wanted to get home so I bought a £208 ticket online.

Later in the afternoon I had a call from Mike Ross in Boswell's office at East Coast. He explained that tickets couldn't be reprinted because of potential fraud but asked me to forward details of my original order and replacement ticket and offered to re-credit my account with the reward points. Ross subsequently emailed me and has committed to credit my account with reward points equivalent to a return journey with a few extra to spare. It was a result of sorts. I would have a return ticket to replace my original single providing that I book in advance within the terms of the East Coast reward scheme. I boarded the 6.30 p.m. to Edinburgh from Kings Cross. Seat 47, coach M. The one I'd originally booked, that I had a receipt for, was empty, of course. I grabbed the reservation ticket as a memento of this story. Everyone who uses social media regularly has a story similar to this one and they'll continue to be created until brands recognise the need to put social communications at their core.

Deeds not words: the suffragettes

Brand vandalism isn't new. It's as old as organisational communications itself. Emily Wilding Davison was a suffragette who died one hundred years ago when she fell under King George V's horse at the Derby. June 2013 was the anniversary of her death. Historians have debated Davison's motivation for running out amongst the horses during a high profile horse race. My view is that she was a brilliant and brave public relations strategist and campaigner.

Davison paid her own way through her education, obtaining first class degrees at St Hugh's College, Oxford, and London University. In 1906 she joined the Women's Social and Political Union (WSPU), founded three years earlier by Emily Pankhurst to campaign through direct action for women's suffrage.

Davison was an incredible woman, who campaigned throughout her life for voting equality using direct action as her means of engagement. She was arrested and imprisoned for various offences on nine occasions. On the night of the 1911 census Davison hid overnight in a cupboard, in the Palace of Westminster, so that she could claim her residence to be the House of Commons. A plaque to commemorate the event was unveiled by Tony Benn MP in 1999.

The 1913 Derby was televised by Pathé News. You can watch the footage on YouTube. My view is that Davison foresaw the opportunity to reach a mass audience for the suffrage cause via news reels shown up and down the UK. A recent reconstruction of the event by a Channel 4 documentary team confirmed that she carefully calculated the location of her action to ensure she secured the attention of the camera. Check out the newsreel and judge for yourself whether or not it was an act of brand vandalism. It was almost certainly a fluke that she collided with King George V's horse mid-race as opposed to any of the other horses, but the story of her campaign would have been reported regardless. A memorial service for Emily took place in St George's Church, Bloomsbury on 14 June 1912. Six thousand women marched through London following her cortege.

The following day her coffin was taken by train to St Mary's Church, Morpeth. As you walk the short distance from the railway station at Morpeth to the rear of the churchyard where Davison is buried you cannot fail to be moved by her story. The inscription on Davison's gravestone reads 'Deeds not words'. Women received the vote on equal terms to men in 1928.

The responsibility of free speech

Free speech online brings with it great individual responsibility. The law is straightforward. You shouldn't defame or slander an individual or organisation. The Jimmy Savile case brought this into sharp focus at the end of 2012. We discussed the Saville case in Chapter 2 in relation to collusion between the media and celebrities. Lord McAlpine, incorrectly identified as a paedophile following the BBC's *Newsnight*, has said that he will pursue a civil case against anyone who defamed him on Twitter.

Prior to McAlpine's action conventional wisdom dictated that it wasn't possible to uphold media law on the Internet. So-called super injunctions, preventing the media from publishing the details of a story, or even the existence of the injunction, have been broken by Twitter users in the past without legal retribution. Twitter is no different to any other form of media from a legal standpoint. The laws governing defamation, slander and decency apply on Twitter just as in any other form of media whether a village notice board or an international news organisation.

Defamation was the charge levelled by Lord McAlpine at the estimated 10,000 Twitter users that wrongly named him as a paedophile and associate of media personality and fundraiser Jimmy Savile, following the botched BBC *Newsnight* programme. The Twitter mob relied on the sheer number of individuals republishing a message and making legal action impossible. But Lord McAlpine's action has brought this mistaken belief to an abrupt end. The Tory peer launched a legal challenge against an estimated 10,000 Twitter users. The vast majority were asked to make a formal apology and donation to charity, while high profile users face litigation. In one case in May 2013, the High Court ruled that a tweet sent by Sally Bercow, wife of the speaker of the House of Commons Speaker John Bercow, was libellous. These cases break new ground and are likely to force attitudes to social media to quickly mature.

The Leveson report published in November 2011 stayed well clear of any attempt to regulate the social media[26]. It acknowledged that the social web is entirely unregulated and that any attempt at online regulation would be problematic because of the tension between national boundaries and the openness of the Internet. Yet the McAlpine case illustrates a desperate and dangerous lack of knowledge about how the law of libel applies to online communications, particularly social media. Basic training in this area is critical for anyone using social media. In fact it should be included as part of secondary school education.

---

26 *The Leveson Report*. http://www.levesoninquiry.org.uk/about/the-report/ (November 2012)

CHAPTER 6

UNDERSTANDING THE ENEMY

How the ire of brand vandals can be turned to a brand's advantage. #BrandVandals

Gold cards and platinum cards are a token of yesteryear's corporate climber. If you want to get premium service today you need to get a TripAdvisor luggage tag. The TripAdvisor luggage tag says, 'I'm active on social networks and a keen reviewer on TripAdvisor.com.' It strikes fear into the heart of restaurateurs and hoteliers the world over. It guarantees good service and upgrades. Organisations are investing huge amounts in building a narrative around their brands. Content in all its forms is the fuel of brand storytelling that engages modern audiences via social forms of media. But as organisations pile into social media they are quickly realising that the old tactics of spewing content out to an audience will only get them so far. Thanks to social networks such as Facebook and Twitter customers can answer back.

The good news is that brands are starting to listen because they have no other option. But guess what? Sometimes the things that customers have to say aren't very nice. On Amazon, Hotels.com, TripAdvisor, to name a few, this manifests itself as lousy reviews. I'm sure I'm not alone in ignoring a restaurant or hotel with less than four stars because there are so many other options.

Social supplants traditional

TripAdvisor shines a bright light on the chasm that exists between modern forms of marketing and customer relationship management. It provides a model for anyone wanting to learn how to manage online feedback. The website, launched in 2000, enables consumers to leave reviews about accommodation, restaurants and visitor attractions. It quickly became the destination location on the Web for travel reviews with more than 60 million unique monthly visitors, and over 75 million reviews and opinions operating in more than 30 countries worldwide. Consumers sign up as members and leave reviews about their experience at places they have visited. Venues are rated for key indicators such as price, value and service.

TripAdvisor has broken all records for the size and scale of its community. It is almost certainly the biggest travel site of its type in the world and has long since surpassed all traditional restaurant and travel guides such as Frommer, Rough Guide and Zagat as arbiters of travel wisdom. It has modernised the travel business by embracing the basic premise of the social web. TripAdvisor's success lies in openness, crowdsourcing and frictionless design of the community. It is very easy to navigate and seek out information and it is equally easy to contribute content in the form of reviews. Reviewers are rewarded with stars and titles based on their activity levels and basic data about how many people have read their reviews. It's a form of gamification aimed at maintaining the interest of community members. Meanwhile mobile versions of the site aim to make it as easy as possible to leave a review.

You know that a area of technology has gone mainstream when your parents adopt it. TripAdvisor passes that test. My mum meticulously checks reviews before visiting somewhere new and always contributes a review on her return. She operates under an anonymous username. Herein lies the chasm in social marketing. How many hotels and restaurants that are busy creating content and building communities of potential customers on Facebook and Twitter take the time to check reviews? If you have a profile in a community or network on the social web you must monitor the activity and in the case of TripAdvisor that can be good and bad.

The other side of the menu

While researching *Brand Vandals* we sought out opinion on review sites such as TripAdvisor from the other side. Comment is hard to come by. Restaurateurs and hoteliers divide into three camps: they get along with TripAdvisor; have a genuine suspicion of the website and its content; or have figured out ways to game the system. Either way there is a very real reluctance for people to share stories from the other side of the fence. The closest we got was a friend from the North-East of England. He is a digital communications manager living in Asia. His wife runs a small restaurant. He had a great insight and was prepared to share with us so long as we withheld his name and the details of his restaurant. The reasons will become apparent as you hear his story and read his comments. I'll call him Jack for the purpose of this interview.

'The general argument in favour of online reviews is that those who are genuinely good will still float to the top. The brand vandals, cranks and the mischief-makers will be drowned out by the well meaning and better informed. For the most part I'd agree but as a digital communications manager with a background in journalism, whose wife runs a small café, I have a foot in both camps. We live and work in a city in Asia. Alongside TripAdvisor we also deal with a local expat review site, which admittedly causes us far more trouble than TripAdvisor. You may at this point be shaking your head and saying that's probably because you're no good. You'd be wrong; we're fourth out of over 300 listed cafés,' said Jack.

Venues run scared of review forums, such as TripAdvisor, because of brand vandals and with good reason. There are members of the community who leave critical reviews. But if a venue's fundamental product and service is sound they should be confident and engage with critical comment. But it isn't easy.

'So, the downsides: well, once a lady claimed she and her family had all ordered lunch and drinks and not one thing was edible and they left it all. She left a one star review. Neither till receipts nor memory helped to recall the lady. You don't forget something like five left meals. We contacted her. She claimed perhaps it was the week before? No it wasn't. Okay then, maybe the month before? No. And so it went on. It was blatantly inaccurate or a fake review,' said Jack.

That one star review remains on the site. At best it is based on a falsehood and at worst it is libellous. Brand vandals hide behind the anonymity of the social web on the one hand and throw around the threat of outing lousy service via review sites on the other.

'We've had a couple of 'What are you going to give me before I review you online?' customers. We first met one gentleman when he turned up at 7 a.m. at a cafe, drunk and covered in sick. He snatched a tea towel to try and clean up the taxi he had vomited in before calmly ordering a bacon sandwich. Some weeks later he returned with his wife waving a piece of paper from the doctor saying she had gastroenteritis, a generic upset stomach, and as she'd eaten there the day before he was demanding $1,000 or he'd write on TripAdvisor. He emptied the place of customers in the meantime, most of which never came back,' said Jack.

You might think that such an allegation wouldn't get past the moderators on TripAdvisor. You'd be wrong. On another occasion, a couple who had arrived in town the day before, ordered a sandwich and were later sick. 'The chances of anyone arriving in this city from overseas and getting an upset stomach is two-to-one odds on. The number of sandwiches we sold that day without one complaint: 30. Hours that food poisoning can take to surface: 48. Did the customers wash their hands before eating? No. Did we complain to TripAdvisor? Yes. Did it make any difference? No. Can you imagine how much that review has damaged our business?' said Jack.

A filter of sceptism

Besides, a slew of positive reviews isn't necessarily a good thing. People, by their nature, are inherently sceptical. A restaurant on TripAdvisor with numerous five star reviews raises my heckles. I'm immediately suspicious as it is either incredibly good, and consistently so, or it is gaming the community. Consistent excellence is rare and inevitably people find fault in even the best venues. Venues have been caught out for breaching TripAdvisor's terms and conditions by getting friends and family to post positive reviews or offering discounts to return customers that leave favourable reviews. It's not smart as they inevitably get caught out.

Jack continued. 'Hotels where I live are in the top five in the world for the quality of their service – according to online reviews. That's because they are in the top position for manipulating or gaming TripAdvisor – it's a local industry, literally. We must be one of the few businesses that neither games the system nor twists arms for reviews. Online review sites do not give you some kind of ultimate truth. One thing that online reviewers rarely realise is that businesses can't delete their review page. There is no opt out,' said Jack.

The TripAdvisor review has become an art form in its own right. Reading through the reviews for a venue it's very easy to spot the contributors with children, the retired couple, and the lone traveller. Each brings their own particular perspective and bias. No venue can please all of the people all of the time. It's now possible to link TripAdvisor to your Facebook network so that you can see reviews from people you know and because I'm aware of their personal preferences I can assign an appropriate bias to their review. This is the latest shift that is taking place in the social web to social search, serving content that is as relevant as possible to an individual.

So people are sceptical of a slew of positive reviews but they are also fair. When people find fault in a hotel or restaurant and share their criticism in a review on TripAdvisor it is beholden on the organisation to accept it as a call to action and respond. Ignoring comment is weak, and frankly rude, especially when that same organisation is trying hard to engage potential customers in communities elsewhere on the social web. An organisation may choose to make changes to its product or service as a result of critical feedback of it may decide that it's fine exactly as it is, but in either case it should respond. People will take this comment on board when making a purchasing decision.

'In the early days we had a couple of occasions when online reviews meant a week long inquest as to what went wrong. Staff were nearly fired or nearly quit. There were tears and recriminations. The customer is always right, right? But no they're not and this has been a lesson for us. When we have good staff we trust them – and we also recognise that staff do make mistakes and we'll apologise for them as required. But we'll also stand up for them sometimes, too. I'd rather lose a bad customer than a good member of staff,' said Jack.

Confrontation by venues doesn't work on TripAdvisor. It frequently appears petty and achieves little. Instead acknowledgement is the best possible response with a one or two sentence response. Likewise, essays don't work. No one will read beyond the first line. Antisocial and snarky behaviour takes place in TripAdvisor every day. It's no different to any other community on the social web. In extreme cases there are mechanisms to report inappropriate behaviour but in the main polite engagement with critics is the best form of defence.

Back chat doesn't work

'We have tried engaging with people. The local expat site allows you to message the reviewers – though they remain anonymous. I've found that most never reply. Of those that do, apart from those whose game is extortion, they rarely want their money back or even to acknowledge your apology. They want to be able to publicly humiliate a business more than they want the problem put right. Sometimes, by engaging, you're just fanning the flames. I believe people are embarrassed when you contact them after a bad review. Having their money returned would mean having to look you in the eye when you hand it over. They see their anonymity as their right and yet they use it to publicly berate you. It is absolutely wrong for only one party to be anonymous,' said Jack.

'Generally if customers want something put right they bring it to the attention of our staff at the time. We don't charge unhappy customers. It's important to realise here that we know we are far from perfect. This is still a developing country. Service levels are generally lower. Local employees encountering foreigners are on a steep learning curve. Suppliers can let us down in terms of quality. Electricity can fail at any time. Heat, dust and pollution have to be dealt with while ensuring hygiene. Our food is good value so it's no frills. The challenges are many and varied,' he added.

Smart organisations use positive reviews from TripAdvisor and other review websites as a means of advocacy and content for their social marketing efforts. Quotes from TripAdvisor find their way into marketing collateral and are shared on the social web. TripAdvisor, for its part, provides venues with marketing collateral showing the rating on the site. These green signs replete with stars are becoming as familiar as more traditional tourist information rating schemes operated by local tourist boards.

Review-based communities such as TripAdvisor need to carefully balance their benefit to users with the value that they deliver to the organisations whose products and services are the subject of review. In the case of TripAdvisor that balance has swung in favour of the user. Tighter community management is required to deal with rogue comments or instances of defamation and slander.

'All businesses are guilty of poor service occasionally and yet sometimes the punishment for this can far outweigh the crime. Trying to engage or reason can put you in the firing line. In the end we've found thick skins are more important than diplomacy or digital communications skills. We've also learned a great deal about managing expectations. Using positive adjectives such as "best", "tasty", and "delicious", are catnip to cranky online reviewers. We don't market anything in that manner now. We play it straight – it's good value and it's fresh. After that people can make up their own minds. We communicate – we don't sell,' said Jack.

There's a final consideration. Each year the traditional travel guides publish top ten lists. These are the best restaurants, hotels and travel destinations, as called by their judges. It's no more than a public relations effort aimed at building the brand or the organisation concerned and flogging more travel guides. The modern TripAdvisor equivalent is dynamic lists created by users of the community using the searches. If you want the best Indian restaurant in London for less than £20 a head, the best hotel in the Lake District for children or the best tourist locations in New York to visit for free, TripAdvisor has the answer.

Troll trouble

Knowing your audience is the first step to engagement. But what if that audience is anonymous and you have no way of identifying its motivation or purpose? The Internet allows anyone to hide behind an online persona and even to create a fake online persona. The low barrier to entry on to the social web has downsides as well as benefits. Individuals can cause huge reputational damage to a brand without being identified or traced. This is an extreme form of brand vandalism called trolling. Trolls are commonplace on blogs and news websites where it is easy to leave anonymous comments and users are able to anonymously vent their fury at stories with which they disagree. Their motivation is power cloaked by anonymity. Head to the *Mail Online* site if you want to see trolling practice raised to an art form. An article on the site about the Duchess of Cambridge's pregnancy received 5,600 comments, which within days were polarised between royalist and anti-royalist.

Such debate and engagement is typically a good thing for newspaper websites but in this instance the speed and hostility of comments was so extreme that comments were switched off. If comments go unchecked then there is no doubt that they will have an undue influence on the audience. That's not just common sense; it's scientifically proven. A recent US study found that negative comments result in readers having negative sentiment about the subject at hand. A hardline moderation policy is typically the key to managing trolls. The challenge is that decency is subjective but it is the role of community managers to set the limits of tolerance. Organisations must balance criticism with outright libel or defamation. Set your policy, make sure you publish it and share it with your community and then police it robustly. This is easily managed on your own social networks and website but when trolls launch fake accounts or pages on networks such as Facebook or Twitter it can take time to work through the processes and procedures that the networks put in place. In almost all cases issues can be resolved without reference to the law. There is no doubt that it is hideous to be the victim of a troll attack, especially if it's personal. Our recommendation is never to fight. Maintain the moral high ground and follow process. This is easier said than done and requires strong leadership but the simple fact is that it's not possible to engage or reason with an anonymous and unknown source.

Google is leading the shift on the social web to real identities rather than nicknames. The identity policy was rolled out as part of Google + in 2011 and requires users to use their proper names rather than an abbreviation or string of characters. Google's premise is connecting people and content on the web via its community and increasingly using social signals in search results. That's made possible using a Google + profile as an identity card that is tied to content that you create and like around the social web. But the real name policy has an additional benefit. Internet users are less likely to engage in antisocial behaviour, such as trolling, if they are using their real identity. The challenge for Google + is policing this rule. It is something that Facebook has failed to do with the result that troll pages are relatively commonplace, particular as a reaction to RIP pages set up to commemorate an individual's death. But so far Google's hardline approach seems to be working and the engagement and quality of conversation on Google + is high.

Courting controversy and clout

Online influence is a tricky business, controversial even. That's because companies want to pin a number on you and create order from the chaotic conversations that characterise social media. Peer analytics firms such as Klout, Kred and PeerIndex, all seek to boil your social media profile down to a single number, or numbers. Identifying which are conversations and which aren't from a single metric is hugely appealing to organisations that are faced with a deluge of conversations.

Real life isn't that simple, of course. To every question there is an easy answer, and there is a right answer. Everyone is influential about something. My teenage daughter isn't going to rank highly on any generic peer analytic metric but based on the conversations she has with friends on Facebook; she's influential about raising animals and horse riding in Northumberland. Organisations are increasingly seeking out influential individuals in their markets as a means of engagement. 'You have to be very careful with whatever you measure, whether it is to be Kred or Klout, to know what you are measuring and what you are seeing. The bigger number does not always point you to the most relevant individual for your brand,' cautions Andrew Grill, CEO, Kred.

The example frequently cited to justify this argument is the UK Prime Minister or US President. You don't have to look too hard to find popstars and celebrities with higher influence rankings according to their Klout, Kred or PeerIndex scores. The bigger number is rarely the right individual. If you want to reach teenage girls who horse ride in Northumberland you know where to come. If your aspirations lie beyond this niche you're going to need to use tools to help identify relevant communities online. Klout, Kred and PeerIndex each has a different business model based around helping organisations identify their communities.

Influence cuts both ways. Tracking the influence of individuals who are discussing your organisation has a second benefit. It enables you to identify the likely impact of your critics so that you can plan and take action accordingly. You may even be able to change their opinion by engaging in conversation and if not you'll have a better understanding of their behaviour and its likely impact on your organisation's reputation.

Grill's firm, Kred, has had access to the full Twitter firehouse since November 2008 and since then has collected, stored and indexed every single public tweet. As of April 2013 that was more than150 billion tweets and growing at a rate of 10 to 20 billion per month. Personal access to your Kred score and Kred Story, a visual history of your Social Media Influence, is free. Unlike Klout and PeerIndex, Kred generates an Influence score and an Outreach score to determine an individual's influence within a market. And unlike its counterparts it is transparent[27] about its rules and how it calculates scores. In fact you're encouraged to look under the bonnet.

Klout rarely engages with individuals on the issue of so-called Klout scores unless it is seeking engagement in a marketing campaign on behalf of a brand. Part of the issue is no doubt scale but it's not clearly unwilling to disclose what goes on in its black box. My repeated attempts to engage with Klout when blogging and writing this book have failed. It's a position that puts it at odds with the social web. It's happy to order and rank people by social graph, boiling individuals down to a number or Klout score, but it won't engage about how it's done.

Kred's openness under Grill's leadership is refreshing. It calculates its Influence metric by how frequently an individual is retweeted, replied, mentioned and Followed on Twitter. If you connect your Facebook account to your Kred profile, you get Influence points when people interact with your content on your wall and the walls of others who have registered their Facebook account. Outreach scores reflect generosity in engaging with others and helping them spread their message on Twitter.

The value of peer analytics tools comes from overlaying these scores against niche markets and identifying the individuals that are influential. Data mining, using proprietary tools, enables bespoke communities based on a market segment

---

27 Kred scoring guidelines, Kred.com, http://kred.com/rules

definition or keyword to be identified and then prioritised using peer analytic tools. This is how Klout, Kred and PeerIndex each ply their trade, using proprietary tools to generate income on behalf of organisations that want to engage with these communities.

Grill believes that Kred's approach of focusing on Influence and Outreach scores sets it apart from its rivals. He describes an assignment for an agency on behalf of a motorsport client. It wanted to find people who were influential in the UK around motorsport so that they could send them on a track day and have them talk about their experience.

'Instead of looking for people who just had the high Influence score, we looked for people who had a high Outreach score. In theory we thought this would work; in practice it worked brilliantly. The agency doing the Outreach said when it contacted people, if they had an Outreach score of 8, 9 or 10 they were really, really interested in being involved; if their Outreach score was below 5 they didn't really care,' said Grill.

Having used a peer analytics tool to identify a community, what next? Engagement puts the public relations industry in a new place. An organisation seeking to engage with influencers within a community needs to play the balance of host and facilitator but also engage with members of the community as equals. Grill says that progressive organisations are starting to treat journalists, bloggers and influencers as equals. It's a brave new world for public relations practitioners used to working with the media as a proxy for engagement with a market.

Critical voices of peer analytics tools aren't hard to find. They claim that it simply isn't possible to rank an individual's influence based on a number and that their approach is simplistic and one-dimensional. Richard Bagnall, Chair of AMEC's Social Media Measurement Group, cites the example of Big Ben in London. It's an automated bot that tweets the 'bongs' of Big Ben every fifteen minutes. At one stage Klout deemed Big Ben to be influential about drugs, presumably based on the content of its tweets and its hundreds of thousands of followers.

Realwire's CEO Adam Parker gets to the heart of the issue. His media intelligence company is building tools such as Lissted to help public relations practitioners understand the conversations that are taking place online among influencers such as bloggers and journalists. Muckrack is doing a similar job for the US market. 'To my mind, tools like Kred, Klout and PeerIndex don't measure influence itself. They do arguably provide some idea of online social capital, part of which is the potential to exert influence. The scores are mostly based on social media data, such as retweets and likes, although they have been trying to build in some real-world context – Klout's recent inclusion of Wikipedia is a particularly innovative example. Remember that many would say that the people closest to us in real life, family, friends and colleagues, are most likely to influence us, and no online tool could realistically measure that. Online measures of social capital, therefore, can only go so far; it is actions and relationships in the real world that are arguably the main components of true social capital.

Real life influence clearly isn't as simple as a single number or even pair of numbers but for now customer service and marketing departments are looking to peer analytics tools to help make sense of the complexity of the social web. Being able to organise and prioritise individuals based on numerical scores is hugely attractive to organisations. 'Relevance and context are also crucial. When you look at Kred, Klout or PeerIndex, it's important to only compare accounts that are already similar– a group of UK-based technology journalists, for example. Kred goes some way to doing this for you, giving profiles a community score instead of a global one, and PeerIndex's recent update includes topic-based scores. Tools like these are developing. Use them, but compare like with like, keep things in context and don't forget a healthy dose of real-world awareness,' said Parker.

Everything Everywhere: turning critics into advocates

When not running Kred, Andrew Grill is an active blogger. As such, he is probably unique as the only influencer platform CEO who has actually experienced the power of influence first hand, something he shares with clients on a regular basis. Grill highlighted issues via the social web with the newly launched Everything Everywhere (EE) 4G mobile network and was then invited to help the company fix its communications issues. We met at the Hospital Club, frequented by London's trendy digital and media types in the heart of Covent Garden. EE, a joint venture between Orange and T-Mobile, launched to consumers with a high-profile advertising campaign in October 2012. On launch day Grill wandered along to the Kensington High Street branch to get a so-called Mi-Fi modem device so that he could take advantage of the promise of superfast mobile broadband.

'I wanted to be one of the first to get 4G so went to line up outside my local EE store. The store opened at 10 a.m. so I was there at 9.50 a.m. hoping that no one would be in the line before me, and as it turned out, there was no line, and so I walked straight in. "Hi," I said to the guy, his name was William, "your lucky day, William, I am going to be your first 4G customer." "Oh great, fantastic," he says. He sat me down, and we went through cheat sheets because it's all brand new, and he starts filling the form out. He turns the screen around and says, "Your application has been rejected,"' said Grill.

Grill had never had a credit issue and assumed that it was an issue with the credit card. He called up EE and was told the problem was due to a change of address over two years before, and their credit scoring provider not having any record of him on file. Instead he called EE's business line, and successfully opened an account and was told he'd be sent a Mi-Fi and SIM the following day. He received the mi-fi modem and a SIM card, plugged it in but could not get connected at all. He called customer services to be told that they were experiencing a high volume of activation and it was likely to take '24 hours'. The next day around the same time he called up again, still not able to connect.

"We've sent you the wrong SIM card, sorry about that. It was a T-Mobile SIM card not an EE one. We'll send you a new one in the post". A new one arrived the next day but it also failed. So that was Tuesday, Wednesday, Thursday. It's now Friday, and they said they'll send me another SIM card. And so on the Saturday I went to my mailbox, got it and it didn't work either. Utterly frustrated by now, I headed back to the store to try to get them to do a SIM swap. William from the previous Tuesday started ringing around the stores to track down stock without success. I was getting fed up now as I had been without service for a whole week,' said Grill.

Grill had tweeted a couple of times during the week about his experience. He'd been variously directed by the EE Twitter account to customer service support at both Orange and T-Mobile, yet he was a brand new Business EE customer, something they were clearly unaware of. Nearing the end of his tether, he headed home and started writing a blog post[28] detailing everything that had gone on. It was a long blog post

---

28 Andrew Grill. *Don't move to 4G on EE just yet – they're not ready for you*. London Calling, http://londoncalling.co/2012/11/dont-move-to-4g-on-ee-just-yet-theyre-not-ready-for-you/ (3 November 2012)

with screen shots and embedded tweets and at 6.30 p.m. he hit 'publish'.

Grill picks up the story.

'I then went off to meet some friends for dinner, and as I'm going up there my phone was buzzing away, with re-tweets, re-posts, and replies. In the first hour I got nearly 1,500 views of the post and probably forty or fifty re-tweets and so I thought I might be on to something. On Monday morning Grill received an email from EE's external public relations company. He emailed back saying he'd like to meet the EE CEO, at which point the internal public relations team got involved. One of their PRs, Howardgot, in touch with Grill and invited him to a meeting at EE's head office. By this point Grill's blog post had caught the attention of the mainstream media, notably the UK's *Daily Telegraph*[29].

On Wednesday Grill headed to EE HQ and was met by the Head of Network, Head of Brand, Head of Social Media, Head of Digital, and Head of PR. The CEO would have been there, too, apparently, but he was in a board meeting next door discussing the issues that I and other customers had highlighted. Grill discovered that EE had supply chain issues. When Mi-Fi modems were being packaged in the warehouse, the wrong SIM was being added. They also had a network coverage issue as a result of merging networks. This was compounded by the Twitter team directing customers to Orange and T-Mobile for support.

'They admitted to me in the meeting that they had launched the network in stealth mode; they had been working on it for 11 months and had told no one, including their staff, and so they

---

29 Christopher Williams. 'EE admits 4G "teething problem" as customers complain of "rush job".' *Daily Telegraph*, http://www.telegraph.co.uk/technology/mobile-phones/9656705/EE-admits-4G-teething-problem-as-customers-complain-of-rush-job.html (6 November 2012)

had just two weeks to train 30,000 staff, and guess what happens when you rush things to market – it doesn't always go to plan. But the most telling thing was they had forgotten about social media. They had two people working on the EE account then; they now have fifty,' said Grill.

Grill persuaded the EE team that they needed to run an advocate programme to get on the front foot and rebuild their reputation. He suggested they should give five advocates a device and data for a year. EE has succeeded in turning a critic into a positive word of mouth advocate. Grill and his fellow advocates are all blogging and tweeting about their experiences. EE has taken a risk but it has also a powerful group of social media supporters for when things are going well and an early warning system for when they aren't.

Social media sleuthing

Brand vandals don't always use social media as a means of attack. Sometimes they quietly sit back lurking on networks such as Twitter to understand an organisation and its motivations. Formula One Ferrari driver Fernando Alonso gave the game away recently in an interview with the *Daily Telegraph* at the end of the 2012 race season[30]. He admitted that race teams monitor social media to understand the configuration of rival cars and morale of teams. Alonso is an avid Twitter user as are fellow Formula One drivers Lewis Hamilton and Jensen Button. They each use social media to draw fans closer to the sport. In Alonso's case he manages his own account in a mix of English and Spanish. But according to him these social media profiles are a useful

---

30 Fernando Alonso. 'Tweeting from the fast lane.' *Daily Telegraph*, http://www.telegraph.co.uk/technology/twitter/9699011/Fernando-Alonso-Tweeting-from-the-fast-lane.html (24 November 2012)

source of entirely legitimate competitive insight as it's hard to hide the problems or stress that a team is facing. If a team is overly optimistic, it's clear there is a problem.

We understand that user-generated content provides a rich source of data for brands to tap. In doing so they are able to understand the motivations of a consumer and determine the best mechanism for engagement. But there are also more ominous applications where organisations are harvesting data and information from social networks for commercial intelligence. This is a voluntary form of surveillance that consumers need to understand. It is unregulated beyond the privacy policies and user agreements for search social media service. Claims investigators in the insurance industry are starting to investigate social media profiles as part of fraud inquiries according to the Coalition Against Insurance Fraud (CAIF). The US organisation says that information can be found on claimants, witnesses, vendors and loss events.

Information that is freely available is generally fair game. Access to a social media profile can be requested in a network such as Facebook where privacy is locked down if the litigant can maintain that it is likely to support a case. Courts are granting access to information if publicly available material suggests that it would be beneficial to a case. In a case in the New York Supreme Court in 2010, a woman named Romana pursued a legal claim against insurance firm Steelcase for its failure to compensate her for injuries that prevented an active lifestyle. The court granted a request from Steelcase to access Romana's social media profiles ruling that preventing access would condone her attempt to hide information behind privacy settings. The court ruled that is was reasonable that her accounts, 'may contain further evidence such as information with regard to her activities and enjoyment of life, which are material and relevant [...].' Steelcase won the case.

In the future it is likely that social media analytics will change the way that investigators use data from social media. Data mining, sentiment analysis and network analysis can already shine a light on activity, good or bad. The next step is to build algorithms that go beyond claim and policy data and scrutinise Facebook friends and Twitter posts.

Journalists have been users of social media from the outset. Tweetdeck is a standard newsroom tool to monitor a breaking story. A new column can be added for each search term or list of Twitter users. Journalists can build lists to monitor conversations around a topic undetected. Twitter enables you to add people to lists without actually following them. It's a technique that any social media sleuth could use. Personal Twitter networks act as informal reporters that will happily share information on request.

Sources themselves can be tracked down using intelligence from Google, LinkedIn and Twitter. Following companies on LinkedIn provides a rich source of information. If you follow a company you'll get a weekly email generated by the network of new hires and leavers, promotions and job advertisements. If you want to go deeper, services such as Duedil in the UK, will scrape annual accounts filings. It is impossible for an organisation to be anything other than transparent about its vital statistics. The reality is that you don't have to work very hard to start to build up intelligence on an individual or organisation using social media.

SECTION 2 – TACKLING BRAND VANDALS

STEVE EARL

CHAPTER 7

DEVELOPING AN EARLY-WARNING SYSTEM

An early-warning system? For more sophisticated and agile threats, try bigger eyes and bigger ears. #BrandVandals

'Sticks and stones may break my bones, but words will never hurt me.' Remember that playground chant, taught to kids by parents wanting them to stand up to bullies and not lash out instinctively if they were called names?

Well the reality is that most brands, since the dawn of industry as we know it today, have largely ignored that advice. They've worked to the assumption that a few words can be extremely damaging. Or have they? To be fair, it's difficult to draw sweeping conclusions. Some brands seem to have an air of high alert about their reputation as affected by the media as we knew it, by public figures, by their competitors and by other stakeholders. Some seem to have had a loose-knit system for dealing with reputational assaults. Most have been somewhere in between – they'd never admit it, but over the years brands have managed negative words about them with an inconsistent mix of oversensitivity and occasional bravado.

This scenario is the overriding reason why, before the advent of the Internet gave rise to two-way media, any 'intruder alarms' that tipped off brands about reputational attacks were bespoke and relied heavily on manual work. What we've seen since social media in particular began to bite as a clear reputational risk zone are many attempts to automate such systematic approaches, enabling – at least in theory – brands to develop an early warning system and take a more rigorous approach to maintaining reputation.

Yet if the vast majority of communications teams were

completely honest on this point, they'd surely concur that they've been locked in a constant struggle to keep pace with the evolution of the threat. Put simply, their ability to keep tabs on new risks as they emerge online has been outpaced by the growing sophistication and severity of those risks.

In practical terms, that has tended to mean patchy visibility over the scope and scale of risks. There have not only been blind spots on the dashboard, but whole features missing in action. In the past, most attempts to consolidate threat information in one place amounted to pulling information from published content in the conventional media and any before-the-event information shared by journalists. Press clippings, transcripts or audio files from radio output and the same from TV. There were always other risks, such as status updates from, for example, public affairs work with politicians, and due process that was in train with regulators, but rarely was all that data consolidated into one single view of reputational risk. At least not formally. Although, when sufficiently smelly poo was about to hit a sufficiently sizeable fan, it would of course be such a priority that the ability to know exactly what a brand was dealing with became utterly crucial.

So what had appeared or was about to appear in the press was typically front and centre, and other peripheral information came from conversations with important influencers that had been captured systematically. As media began fragmenting and expanding in the 1980s and early 1990s, that operational challenge grew larger – there were simply more outlets to keep an eye on. Early warning systems of a sort evolved, but the increased sophistication was largely restricted to the ability to share raw and recent information by email rather than by phone or fax.

What we've seen for the past 10 years or so, since blogging began to become more prevalent and communicators developed initial awareness of social media, is an ongoing attempt to add greater visibility by extending the press dashboard into something that can drill into social and owned media too. All too often, though, the drilling doesn't go far enough, so the view of risk remains too narrow.

Media relations has been the primary form of reputation management since the 1950s. Change is slow and there is lots of evidence to suggest that the current generation of communications practitioners don't even see new forms of media as part of their remit. Or if they do, they only really scratch the surface of keeping on top of threats as they develop.

And even if the vast majority of the information could be pulled together and assessed, the systems tended to have a major flaw – the ability to act rapidly and systematically upon that information. In many cases, the reliance on hope was a major factor in the early warning system mix.

That's not because the risks weren't there, they just weren't as immediate or as potent. Regardless of the extent to which brands felt relatively shielded from the effects of negative words and pictures or persistently exposed, and regardless of their capability to deal with sabotage efforts, most have long had a level of concern about what others say about them. And about the effect that issues that flare up in the public eye may have on causing them short-term harm, or long-term destruction. They may have systems and people for tackling every stick and every stone, but know that words can wound, and some can even be fatal.

Beginning in the mid-1990s, and advancing rapidly in the wake of social media scandals that have shown large organisations how exposed they can be to a new generation of reputational attacks, levels of sensitivity about how individuals or groups can trash a reputation very quickly have been growing. Not just growing, actually, but mushrooming into what can become hyper-sensitivity, with communications teams instructed to build higher reputational defences against a rising tide of communications activism. The immediacy of the Internet has shown the degree of exposure that can exist, and the speed with which negative feeling and information can spread. And how the digitised media environment can spread misinformation just as quickly, if not faster, than the accurate stuff.

The nasty people out there are looking at brands can see more than they ever could before, can be better organised to strike and can be stirred into action with greater vitriolic bile than ever. Whereas in the age when the evening TV news was the pinnacle of potential embarrassment or reputational knocks, today the sheer pace of assault, emotional snowballing and a new breed of munitions can combine to make brands feel like they're facing the rampaging armies of Attila the Hun armed with little more than a customer enquiry helpdesk, wit and charm.

The nasty people can not only look menacing; they can be an invisible menace that is, unless they've done some serious law-breaking, impossible or unfeasible to track down.

As organisations get to grips with media change and many brands become much more innovative in managing their reputations not just in areas of new media, but in an integrated fashion across all media forms, their ability to respond to vandalism is, technically, ever-better. On paper at least. But the ability to protect against brand soiling is becoming something of an arms race, a war of attrition borne of the new age of immediate, transparent engagement with audiences that the Internet has enabled, and a stirring in the digital loins of detractors who want to do brands harm.

Being new-media savvy and having managed to tackle some big communications crises in the past simply isn't enough these days, and you can bet that the reputational war will continue. Brands need early warning systems that give them eyes in the backs of their heads. Anything other than full disclosure leaves blind spots, and blind spots can leave enemies drooling.

Can we learn from history?

It's still bad stuff said or unearthed by 'bad' people, though, isn't it? Surely if we can up the pace and get a grip on the volume of content now swilling around, we can build a bigger shield?

Perhaps. But probably not. Before looking to the future, it's worth looking back at how brands have aimed to gain that early warning advantage in the past, as some techniques may still apply and will continue to be useful.

One of the big changes that the Internet, egged on by social media, has brought to the world of journalism is the disappearance of the deadline. Today's news deadlines are as soon as the button on the keyboard can be pressed, but think back to how media output was charted in the less frenetic days of regular, 24-hour news cycles.

The average person's day began with the morning news. Way back before things could be sent through the air invisibly, that meant a morning newspaper, delivered to an address for consumption there or purchased from an outlet and read, typically, while in transit. Then came radio, and the dawn of the news bulletin – pre-scheduled snippets of prioritised news with the occasional newsflash and more in-depth discussion features worked into the programming schedule. Television followed this lead, but its ability to show moving pictures could make the impact more profound, and gave brand detractors a new weapon to play with.

Process could ensure that the content of the morning news was captured, reviewed and could form the basis of what recommended action was deemed appropriate.

Throughout an average day, further news bulletins appeared in the broadcast media, and negative stories that developed would build up a head of steam, so that by late afternoon the following morning's newspapers would be planning their next round of coverage. Evening newspapers were a factor, too, but could be folded into the same monitoring approach.

In the case of major corporations, sophisticated processes were typically developed and tuned over the years, although many relied on a combination of automated tracking and information provisions from third parties and manual trawl, typically consolidated and presented in the form of bulletins and, where necessary, newsflash alerts and emergency action mapped out. Those close-of-day status reports tended to circulate only news coverage that was predicted to include a brand or would be of commercial interest to the brand. Otherwise, dinner-time, evening TV and a cheeky glass of wine or two went largely undisturbed.

Unless the frantic search for fact and spokespeople who were available to talk to media interrupted such fireside plans. Sound familiar?

Times have changed. Today the systematic sharing of just-published and predicted news output still needs to happen, and is still absolutely relevant to the brand's reputation and the business at large. But the systemic, clockwork scheduling of such bulletins is no longer relevant – today, the deadline is simply as soon as is physically possible. The time to look out for it is within a split-second of an authorised somebody pressing the send button.

But while systematic sweeps of the media by communications teams remain prudent, the basis of them needs to evolve from how they were conducted in the past to why they need to be conducted today: it now needs to be predominantly about judgement, rather than mostly about luck – luck in that while sound editorial judgement was typically employed, much of the process was manual and what was published was in the hands of the media, with the brand having zero direct control.

In the past, those sweeps for news output were like a radar operator searching for known or enemy aircraft with one eye shut. When stories – even major, risky stories – broke they tended to be picked up because the communications teams were looking for them, and waiting nervously for them to appear in print or be aired. But sometimes, they were found by accident during a casual sweep of media outlets. And sometimes they could be missed altogether and spotted by someone else within the organisation, by which time the train may have already left the station as the story had already broken in the media.

Because while communications teams needed to respond quickly or really quickly to breaking news that posed them risk, quickly didn't usually mean immediately. Normally, there was some wriggle room, even if that wriggling could well cause some metaphoric chafing. Luck may not have been a central part of the strategy, but invariably it was part of the mix.

Today's early warning systems need to be precision-engineered to be anchored firmly on sound communications principles, driven by commercial priorities and orchestrated with clear, non-emotive judgement. They need to have assessed how the audience is likely to react – or how it's already reacting – and those assessments need to have been made already, so that they're waiting in the wings. They need to have seen the myriad of paths to potential brand harm or ruin. They need to have charted every millimetre of those paths, sniffed the morning air and have computed every potential eventuality. Every possible avenue or cul-de-sac on the road to brand sabotage needs to have been scrutinised and mapped.

Needs to, but won't have been. Because it's utterly unrealistic, of course. Human beings are human beings, plus no two situations are totally alike.

But the point is more that attitudes must change. Communications teams mustn't wait to see if they're lucky so that hopefully judgement day never comes. Judgement and data need to be baked in to the process.

So what's missing?

At the risk of sounding flippant, a lot of the 'early' and quite a bit of the 'warning'. The point is that while most brands have some sort of system in place to monitor what's said and written about them in public, and typically that will be prioritised around the outlets and channels that have the potential to cause them the most damage, many struggle to move fast enough. They need to spot and tackle the content earlier, before things turn nasty. Or if they're nasty from the off, they need to be even faster to act.

And while the systematic approach can ensure warning is given appropriately, that warning can only be effective when a sweep is made of all applicable outlets and channels. That's tough to do when every day many new ones crop up, existing ones add new features to their formats and others wither on the vine. In short, it is a very big, global moveable feast that continues to grow, and that can leave a lasting trail on the Internet for all to see. To be able to provide adequate warning, the system needs to be able to see every threat.

Thankfully, the flipside of the level of immediate reputational threat that the Internet has caused is that digital content and the process of publishing it leaves an audit trail, so it is possible to use tools and services to gain that visibility, assemble the right data and compile it into a dashboard-like format for monitoring the lot. That way, alerts and warning processes can be triggered. While in the case of sophisticated attacks by brand detractors the tracks will have been covered, so determining who published it and where may be tough or impossible, at least you can see what you're dealing with. The challenge is that there's just so very much to deal with.

Things are improving, though. As monitoring services expand their reach, so there will be fewer places to look, and standardised practices for gathering the data will develop further. The level of reach required is daunting, but it's possible to attain it, even if part of the work has to be done manually. So with the right brainpower in place to know what needs to be done in order to respond quickly, brands can get to grips with all of this and gain that all-important super-agility, right? Wrong. Because one problem remains; a central challenge and very necessary part of the process that can all too often be the Achilles' heel of timely external communications: authorisation.

When the whole brand, or the entire organisation, needs to make a statement, it can get stage fright. Or the person at the top can be in a meeting from which they simply can't be extracted. In the age when being late with responses to reputational attacks just isn't an option, and moving fast can and often does make the difference between a molehill being made into a mountain in brand damage terms, the person or people in charge need to say yes or no to the words or pictures that will come out of the brand's 'mouth'.

That person may not be at the very pinnacle of the organisation either, which complicates things further. Many brands give autonomy over how they communicate to the communications team, yet in the instance of an act of deliberate, and perhaps malicious, and even illegal vandalism against a brand's reputation, the parent company and either divisional or 'topco' lawyers are likely to need to gather around the problem quickly. Although rarely can that be done quickly enough to avoid at least reputational bruising, if not a lasting wound.

The missing element doesn't tend to be seniority, but cohesion. Without that cohesive approach across the brand, or the organisation, or the operational functions – or all of those areas – it's difficult for sound decisions to be made and nigh-on impossible for them to be made in time to stem the flow of blood. Even where it can be done, it can occupy so much of those people's time that it can become a damaging distraction in its own right. There needs to be a single process – an extensive process – that everyone has agreed to and everyone is posed to act upon when needed. Silos can't exist.

There's another element that tends to be missing from these processes and it's an important one, particularly given the pace of media evolution in the world today. It's that in dealing with brand sabotage, and particularly with less severe incidents, brands need to learn from their mistakes and from what they do when they handle situations well. And if they're smart, from how others handle their own brands.

Early warning systems are at their best when they leave no stone unturned in assessing threats, have the function required to respond and engage immediately and are organic, in that they are constantly evolving and improving.

Because brand vandals are always evolving and improving themselves. You can't prevent them from doing it, but with some well thought out, built-in protection, vandalism can at least be contained and acknowledged. And even, perhaps, used for reputational gain.

Can you really see everything?

Well, perhaps we were a little hasty a few paragraphs ago by inferring that monitoring continues to get better and so bad stuff can always be seen. In fairness, a lot of it can. Equally, even if you don't know where to dig there will always be blind spots, and always things that didn't appear to be threatening at first glance. While many have critiqued the claim, Google's Eric Schmidt has said that we're now adding as much new content to the Internet each day as we did from its invention to 2003[31]. And Eric should know, shouldn't he?

But wading through all of that content to assess potential acts of vandalism is tricky, whatever the monitoring capability. Take Facebook for example: you can't simply keep looking for brand mentions and relevant topics. Saboteurs may just go for your throat, but equally the threat could stem from something more innocent that they then picked up, twisted and used against you. How could you have seen that coming? It could crop up on a page that has very few friends and connections, but the issue could get spotted and then used against you.

Context and nuance can help you to assess the threat, but even so it's a struggle. The best way to look at all of this, and so to plan a systematic approach to dealing with it, is to imagine that the whole world of published content can be seen, but not all of it in the same sharp focus. More popular and mainstream media, and more glaring threats, should be crystal clear. Dim threats will become apparent quickly as they come to the fore.

No matter how out of focus they appear, sooner or later, all threats will pop up on the 'grid'. Which means they become ones and zeroes. And just like Arnold Schwarzenegger in *Predator*, when he said of the alien, 'If it bleeds, we can kill it', if it's digital we can track it. Ideally all in the same place.

Media monitoring can't be left to machines alone, however. Many of the world's biggest brands have done much in recent years to formalise their round-the-clock, clinical monitoring of content published about them, supported by a clear process.

---

31 M G Siegler, 'Eric Schmidt: Every 2 Days We Create As Much Information As We Did Up To 2003,' *Tech Crunch*, http://techcrunch.com/2010/08/04/schmidt-data/ (August 2010)

And as those processes continue to get stretched by media change and the ingenuity of reputation saboteurs, so monitoring requires a strong steer from human beings, even if it's computers that do the trawling.

There's one obvious place to tune that listening ear in order to second-guess where threats might come from: the enemy. Any and all organisations that have expressed their distaste for a brand's activities, their vehement opposition or even their slight disdain are candidates for either constant alert monitoring or at least to have a watchful eye kept on them. How can that best be done? Well, the topics of interest and relevancy to your brand will typically be the same ones that 'the opposition' is all over. Beyond that, the same principles apply as in the age of media relations when brands would monitor their competitors' press clippings in order to work out who was getting the most exposure, and what they might be missing out on. Only now, the reputational stakes are far higher and the requirement goes much further than comparative analysis.

The bottom line, though, is that the vast majority of potentially harmful content can be seen, assessed and – with adequate, agile and adaptive due process – cut down to size. It can potentially even be turned into a positive, or at least create some sympathy, for the brand. Reputation can't be controlled, it can only be commanded, and there is a jungle of conversation out there.

It pays to be well equipped in a jungle, as it can be full of nasty surprises.

View from the top

Ultimately, the people who are probably most in the firing line are not the brand managers but those with overarching responsibility at the top of the organisation. While brand managers are the ones having to tackle the challenges head on, it's the people at the top who risk taking the biggest fall. Should they expect the communications team to do more to protect them?

Well how would they know what to expect? One consistent theme of the Internet's rise to prominence as the biggest forum for reputational risk is that each new scandal or act of brand trashing shocks onlookers with its severity, speed and scale. The rules have been re-written, and it's easy to see why the expectations of senior management may not be aligned to such new threats.

There are no precedents for this. There isn't a clear, pre-ordained way to deal with situations that could have been anticipated. And in many cases, not enough has been done to shield reputations from the broad and deep impact of potential attacks. The important thing for those at the top to appreciate, if they haven't done so already, is that this stuff ranks alongside the most serious situations that they have or will ever face in their positions of responsibility. Not literally life and death, but certainly the life or death of the brand.

This is a process as important as any personnel procedure, stock exchange requirement, building regulation or compliance process. It could mean the life or death of the business or the brand. And those other things are board-level issues that have exceptionally costly consequences. So does your reputation. It is that simple.

It's difficult to see how else to illustrate the severity of getting it wrong or failing to tackle problems of this magnitude. Sustained reputation protection needs attention at a senior level, from the top down. Not just attention, but buy-in, under-standing and continued commitment.

In many organisations these days, it does seem that the impact on reputation of content published on the Internet has become a board-level issue. But that's not really the point here: being an acknowledged issue is one matter; having board-level ownership of sustained measures that are taken to bolster defences against attacks or move clinically to quash incidents and tackle illegal behaviour when it occurs is another. Executives need to buy into whatever the agreed approach and processes are, understand the risks and implications and ensure that the organisation is investing continually in doing all it can to be prepared for incidents. And when incidents occur, it can be smart about what action to take.

That means that the board must appoint and authorise others to act. While the decision on how to deal with attacks, depending on their severity, may rest at board level, there must be clear rules of engagement, with teams and individuals given designated responsibility for responding to provocation. That empowerment to act must be handed out in advance, because if it's left until an incident is in progress, it's likely to be too late to be effective.

How that chain of command functions will of course depend on the business, the charity or the government department in question. Usually, an agile and clever response is best driven by one individual having overall responsibility for seeing through the planned actions that have been determined by the board – or for less severe incidents, that individual can act without board referral. That person can then further delegate specific responsibilities to teams of people to act within agreed confines in order to listen, plan, develop content, and engage with stakeholders and audiences in order to communicate and monitor what happens as a results. Those teams may be drawn from departments as diverse as human resources, product development, finance, research and development, communications and, of course, legal.

The people at the top of the tree don't necessarily need to be in the spotlight at all. Depending on the nature of the incident, they may not even need to get involved. But in all cases they should be kept informed, with a full and frank assessment of risk shared with them frequently as it evolves.

And what should the all-important flow chart look like for responding and gaining command over vandalism situations? Well there's no one-size-fits-all plan, obviously. Scale of attack, market context, incident specifics, nature of the industry, commercial priority at that point in time and many other variables will combine to determine what needs to be done and in what order. But knowing how you intend to respond to a variety of foreseeable incidents of any level of severity is the important thing. Like a public building or facility that needs people and equipment on permanent standby, and then uses set, information-led processes to determine a course of action, the key thing is to be prepared, and indeed to be prepared for any eventuality.

Think of any high-risk and high-security environment, like a central bank or an airport. A team is always on alert, with the authorisation and the ability to respond, and both of those environments are geared to handle the most severe kind of situation imaginable, if it ever happens. Information is always at a premium in a bid to identify incidents before they become bigger incidents, and to foresee them before they even become incidents by continually assessing recognisable patterns of behaviour or data. Less like being able to see around corners; more like having eyes in the back of the head. And at the sides.

Unlike physical premises and the contingency plans that are drawn up in the interests of public safety or commercial security, determining how best to protect and act to defend the interests of reputation is tied to an understanding of the audience and knowing the truth. The audience – both the immediate audiences and the broader public – and how they are likely to perceive both the act of brand sabotage and your response to it will have a significant bearing on the chosen course of action.

To that end, already being closely engaged with the audience online is a big help.

But there is no greater factor than the truth. If activists make public something that is fact, something that you had wished to keep confidential, and if that fact has negative consequences for your audience or the broader public, then look out. Your task is probably to minimise damage, rather than to right a wrong. If what activists have claimed is actually untrue, you have an entirely different situation on your hands.

It may sound blindingly obvious, but you'd be surprised how many times, both when responding to online communications and to other crises offline, that the most fundamental question isn't asked right at the beginning of the process: So, is this true?

But with those facts established, and a firm grasp on what the audience is likely to – or does – think, then the best way to arm the brand is to be utterly prepared. With no stone left unturned. Sound planning, the greatest degree of visibility attainable and the foresight that comes from learning from the mistakes and successes of the past means that practically any situation can be tackled, and turned around.

Modern skills for modern threats

So it all sounds pretty simple, doesn't it? Get your act in gear, be pragmatic about who does what and get organised to military levels and you can build your brand Batfink-like wings of steel.

Well it would be very simple, if it weren't for the one thing that does most to undermine efforts to respond positively to communications crises. The one thing that the vandals are trying to sway in the first place.

People.

Much has been written about the skills that corporate and government communications teams must possess in the Internet age. The dawn of popular social networking sites like

Facebook promoted a rush of digital teams or communicators to come to the fore, who professed to have the skills to be able to tackle online reputation crises. Perhaps many did, but the fact that the medium is digital is not the point here. What it comes down to is that the Internet has accelerated the need to respond quickly beyond all known recognition, forced complete transparency and lowered the bar of editorial entry to near-zero. It means communications teams do need some new skills to be able to deal with this changed media environment, but they need to sharpen up their acts across the board too. There's nowhere to hide, and no room for comfort.

Jonathan Copulsky, a principal at consulting firm Deloitte, one of its top experts on customer relationships and author of the book *Brand Resilience*, puts forward these fundamental requirements. 'Clearly, communications teams need sensing capabilities so that they can detect online attacks in their early stages. These sensing capabilities need to combine technology enablers with human intelligence to help gauge severity and urgency of attacks, lest the team waste efforts and time chasing "ghosts". In addition, communications teams need to include individuals responsible for reaching out to and activating internal and external ambassadors, who can, in turn, help disseminate key messages through social platforms,' he said.

There's a long list of skills required, as well as a large dose of common sense. Here, though, are six types of skill that the modern communications team should develop and continue to improve in order to be effective. None are new, but all are fundamental, and need to be stretched beyond the bounds of the era of print and broadcast, these being the primary forms of media.

Firstly, organisation. The way communications is orchestrated in order to tackle brand vandalism must be rooted in military-like procedures, so that everyone knows their role and there is a place for everything. Procedures, multiple paths of action mapped to foreseen circumstances, content production, revision and approval, and the people who need to come together to make it all happen must be corralled into one cohesive, progressive function. Communications must be precision-engineered, with the assumption being that there is absolutely no margin for error; a science, not an art, although the organisation must give scope for creativity, for guile and for instinct. Attaining the right level of attentiveness is something that can only really be done by highly organised people, and that's the first fundamental skill of today's communicator in tackling reputational threats. And then there's ingenuity; but more of that later.

Having ironed out any rough edges that existed, overcome weak spots and brought order where only limited process existed, there must also be recognition that the early warning system is not an indomitable machine that must just be polished and admired. It must also be inherently pliable, so that it can adapt quickly and with minimal effort to any change in immediate circumstance, as well as to evolve progressively as media continues to become more sophisticated and brand or commercial priorities change. Adaptability, or rather, a lack of it, can be the biggest blind spot for brands needing to maintain constant vigilance. Like any arms race, the enemy will simply observe your defences at close quarters, study them, innovate and then try to hit you with something that you have no real answer for. You've simply got to keep building the wall higher and better. But you've also got to keep a permanent watch on the media environment: only by charting media change and understanding the implications of new technologies and new techniques for your master plan will you achieve the level of protection that the brand really needs. Adaptability may be a consequence of good planning and organisation but again it takes people who are, at heart, adaptable beings to make things function that way; people who never feel comfortable resting on their laurels. Adaptability is the second skill.

And to sound like a stuck record, the people running the system and who are involved in every aspect of the communications function have to be extremely agile. There are effectively no deadlines, as it's a case of as soon as is physically possible. Agility is the third skill. We're not robots, though, and human beings can only move so fast in order to react. So the underlying support system and pre-approved plan needs to enable them to move as fast as they possibly can. All too often the system, the tools and the bureaucracy slow people down, rather than giving them the ability to deliver at optimum speed.

The support system also relies on them not freaking out, getting distracted by irrelevant details, making errant decisions or undershooting on the intentions of the communications just because the pressure is on. It's understandable, again because we're just human, that the immediacy and transparency of the Internet leaves brands and their guardians exposed, so communicators have to work under tangible pressure in order to do their jobs. The ability to stay calm, therefore, is the fourth type of skill that they need. They've always had to do that, but the need has never been greater. Remember when monthly magazines gave you 10 days to respond to a request for information? Well, compare that with an act of sabotage, which means that 100,000 more people are seeing and sharing problem content every 10 minutes, so that before the day is out a sizeable chunk of the developed world's population may be aware of 'your story'. Calmness is not just a virtue, it's an essential ingredient. Perspective, rather than panic, is required in order to carry out plans with flair, and with sound judgement.

You've probably guessed, then, that these people are going to need to be brave, too. Not brave like fire-fighters, racing drivers or shark fishermen, but brave within the context of the communications profession. And actually, given how high the stakes, are, acts of vandalism call for a type of valour that's rarely seen in the regular corporate world. Sure, the people calling the biggest commercial shots out there have to live by their wits and show guts to make tough decisions. But the decisions and actions of communicators may have equally sweeping consequences, and the whole world may be watching as they make them. Communicators today must stick to their guns when faced by the gravest of reputational challenges. While they're hardly superheroes, they nevertheless must be strong in the face of internal panic and refuse to be drawn by detractors.

And finally, communicators must be ingenious. Because even when presented with the most tortuous of sabotage incidents, they have an opportunity to gain cut-through and take the advantage for the brand. Doing so will require a team that is organised, adaptable, agile, calm and brave, but beyond that success can be driven through ingenuity. The ability to disrupt and diffuse situations by knowing how the audience and the vandal are likely to react to your actions, then using collective brainpower and creative strategies to outmanoeuvre the opposition, is what can set one communications team apart from another, or from all the rest.

Copuslky sets out a similar list of priorities in *Brand Resilience*:

- Undertake a thorough assessment of potential internal and external risks (much like one might inspect a home for fire-related risks) and consider what defences to put in place.
- Educate 'the troops' (i.e. the employees) to help them understand the potential for brand sabotage and allow them to identify potential brand-damaging incidents before they get out of hand.
- Build early warning systems or sensing capabilities to detect attacks in the early stages.

- Rehearse responses to potential attacks so that everyone understands their role and responsibilities in responding (much like fire drills).
- Thoroughly analyse what went well (and what went poorly) with each attack so that the brand can learn and adapt its response for the next attack.
- Measure impact of attacks and track over time.
- Create the internal and external ambassadors who can be activated to help respond to problems when they happen.

It's all about being forewarned and having the capability to deal with a more sophisticated and more agile threat. Effectively, you need to be able to see their level of brainpower, and you can raise them by beating them at the game they've started. It is like reputational chess played on crack.

CHAPTER 8

GETTING ON THE FRONT FOOT

Make it harder for mud to stick. Keep your reputation shield polished. #BrandVandals

The audience priorities of an organisation are changing because of media change. This is having a big impact on the way in which brands communicate: not just how they orchestrate that communication across media new and old, but how they plan it, how they react to new information and how they listen to the reactions of others.

More progressive brands have realised that the rules of the audience identification and mapping game have changed. Audiences no longer sit in discrete camps without talking to each other. Of course, they never really did, but now the ability of those groups to influence each other as well as individuals to influence each other is strikingly clear. From shareholders to customers, from managers to suppliers, from employees to customers and from policymakers to compliance managers, one fact is now front and centre of how brands plan to tell stories about and relevant to themselves, and how they look to protect themselves from the finger-pointing of others. It is that you simply can't say one thing to one group of people, and something else to another. You'll be rumbled.

By understanding how media has changed and the requirements that that places upon communications and by building a strong reputation a brand puts itself in a position of strength, organisations stand a much better chance of dealing with attacks of vandalism. The question is what they need to do consistently to counter the threat and to be on the front foot, rather than standing on the back one waiting to be knocked over. Equally, communicators need to always be mindful that brands aren't really tangible things; they're phenomena that exist purely in the hearts and minds of the audience.

Is your audience really the world?

A great early warning system that evolves continually to counter threats is a huge asset, then. But it's also important to consider who really cares about the bad stuff that brand detractors may want to spread. Put bluntly, you may not care too much what some people think or say about you, but surely there are a lot of people who you do care about, and a smaller group of people whose views are absolutely crucial.

There are many ways in which audiences can be segmented, and before the Internet came along this tended to be done along fairly classic lines. Sure, priorities are always bespoke, but there were overarching themes common to the vast majority of brands. Important audience groups were people who bought things from you, were your partners in selling things, impacted the market in which you operated, worked for you and advised others on the goods or services you provided. All had tangible importance in the commercial success of the organisation and could be considered primary audiences for brand communications. Priorities would vary and could shift around depending on seasonal factors and changing needs, but those groups tended to be addressed as individual groups and in priority order. In some cases there was personal engagement so the communication was more of a dialogue, but many people were spoken at, rather than to.

Consistency was an important factor in ensuring that the brand was never accused of being divided over its focus, intentions or loyalties, but could quickly evaporate in the event that audiences overlapped or compared notes.

In the past, you couldn't control what those groups of people thought, but you could control how you told them things – well, not control, but at least try to command, through media relations. The immediacy and transparency of the Internet has changed that. Today more so than ever, organisations need to see the audience of a brand holistically, as one large audience, while maintaining clear focus on the information needs and expectations of a long list of discrete audiences groups. There needs to be a consistent overall story, but it needs to go further for each of the interest groups you're telling it to. And there needs to be a range of techniques for tackling unwanted interruptions.

In effect, the audience of any brand these days is a global audience. It is potentially every man, woman and child on the planet. Regardless of whether a brand operates in a country under a different brand name or doesn't want its audience to be global, that fact is that it is global. Because so is the Internet.

But that's a big audience, and hardly targeted. It needs to be considered by brands in their planning because no one can be completely kept away from information any more (well, apart from in a few dictatorships, but even then information democracy seems to find a way through). The assumption has to be that anyone and everyone can potentially read or listen to your content, although the reality is that a much smaller section of the global population, in the case of most brands, is the group you really want to build and protect reputation with.

It's perhaps better, once the audience groups have been segmented and prioritised, to look at overall reputation management and the work that's needed to counter attacks by distinguishing passive audiences from ones that are actively engaged. That engagement doesn't necessarily mean a sustained level of feedback or fascination, but a professed or a likely interest in the brand and its activities, either because those people buy from you or are connected to your commercial activity, or because they buy from your competitors. Because an engaged audience won't necessarily just be made up of people who like you and like the brand. Though those people are nonetheless very much part of your audience, the reality could be quite the opposite.

The end of the line

It's often said that the Internet has democratised so much in the world. It has certainly changed the game on many fronts. For political activism, see the Arab Spring in North Africa. For swifter shopping decisions, see retail price comparison sites. For rapid sharing of breaking news – although the facts can often go astray in the process – see the enormous number of online news sources.

Barriers have been broken down. Not just the erosion of restrictions that previously occurred in the real world, but practical barriers that existed between audiences and the tools through which brands communicated with them. Often, those barriers may have been artificial but brands tried to stick to them nonetheless – sometimes to their chagrin. Think of the case of sensitive, confidential information that has to be or is deemed to be appropriate to be shared company-wide through an internal communications exercise with the insistence that it's kept secret until the time comes for it to be shared publicly. In all but the most sensitive of organisations where employees felt a strong moral obligation or an acute legal requirement to keep quiet, the risk of someone squealing tended to be ever-present. Hence many such initiatives being internally dubbed Project Dynamo or similar, with a communications team committed to keeping the detail to strictly a need-to-know basis – right up to the point where someone who's agitated or has taken leave of their senses decides to blab and the whole thing blows up in their faces.

In recent years we've been coming to the end of the road for the line drawn between internal and external audiences. We've also seen lines blur, diminish or cease to exist between the way external audiences used to be communicated with as discrete groups.

The end of the line for boundaries is just one factor we have to tackle in working out how to get on the front foot. Another big consideration is that no matter what you do, how quickly you think, act or counteract the information that's posted online about your brand, your audience can move way faster than you. Because they have the same tools, and there are a lot more of them.

That can feel really oppressive for brands, but if you think about it, it's a scenario that simply reflects the real world. For a long time, in the era of media relations and discrete offline communications to chosen audiences, brands had the luxury of time to think and react. They could treat audience groups as one big amorphous blob. But the way that the Internet enables personal communication, so that billions of individuals potentially can communicate with brands directly, has put a stop to all that. There are no real boundaries any more, and brands have to communicate with the audiences both en mass, as smaller groups and as individuals. And above all as human beings.

It's just that there are lots and lots of human beings. Ones who like you, ones who are ambivalent and ones who definitely don't like you. And they can move very quickly to harm your reputation on a global scale.

So it's no wonder that confidentiality can be very hard to come by, and in many cases it's almost better to assume that it's impossible. Secrecy and discretion have worn very thin, perhaps because the audience feels there are no longer any real lines to breach. Certainly expecting significant or sensitive information to be retained within an organisation for a long period of time before its external communications can be carefully orchestrated seems only a memory now. There are still external and internal audiences, but there is no longer really external and internal communications, at least not as we knew it.

How can brands turn these modern communications routes to their advantage, then, rather than be at the whim of a boundless audience where anyone can suddenly be informed or react, whether you like it or not? Well, it all starts with a stark acknowledgement that while brands have to be prepared to talk at and respond to absolutely anyone, their planned communications needs to be focused on the people who will really create influence or who they have duty to inform. Talk to any, but converse with a few.

You can speak directly to an individual, but they may share the information. But rarely today can you speak directly to a group; you have to assume you're speaking to everyone. However, you can tailor the content of your conversation to the people who you really want to talk to by focusing on things that really interest them – or use deliberate ploys to prompt engagement or reaction from others you wish to involve or dismiss.

And equally, brands have to be prepared for detractors to butt in to their orchestrated conversations with their priority target audiences. Of course, there can be members' only forums like LinkedIn groups, user forums and circulation lists restricted to known individuals. But unless it's illegal, immoral or personally unwise to do so, there is always a risk that information intended to be the privy of a few will be circulated to others – who you can't control – around the world.

Whereas in the past sharing information may have taken some effort, today it can come down to the pressing of a finger on a small button.

A reputational shield

So let's come to the crunch. Brands need some protection from this, and to build defences around themselves to – if you'll permit the military analogy – take up a position on higher ground so they're more likely to spot the enemy's first move and make it easier to hold their position.

In fact, brands may feel they're forever on the defensive, but with a smart defence network they can actually even go on the offensive. If they need to.

By engaging and setting expectations amongst the audience that they really want to engage with, brands stand a better chance of building trust, belief and ultimately unequivocal faith with their audiences. All of those factors may be relatively fragile, but the more of them they have in their arsenal, the more effective the reputational shield.

However, it goes well beyond simply having a lot of people interested in the brand, or having chosen to follow or like it on social networks. Just because someone has chosen to receive information over the Internet about the brand or expressed their favour for it doesn't mean they necessarily have a strong emotional tie with it, will maintain a strong belief that it will do or provide things that are useful or desirable for them or indeed give much of a toss about its fortunes. While the world of marketing has been in hot pursuit of the holy grail of engagement for several years now, just because you've been hooked in doesn't mean you're paying much attention or really care. And you could always wriggle off the hook.

Engagement with members of the audience who are not only positive about the brand but are likely to remain supportive of it through thick and thin needs to go deeper than simply having some kind of functional digital connection. All that has done is overcome the supposed or entirely hopeful effect of advertising and other forms of brand or product promotion. Think of it like a football ground or any other passionate sporting stadia: just because it's pretty much full of people doesn't mean you'll necessarily hear the persistent roar of passionate support. Just because you've done a swift trade in replica shirts and scarves doesn't mean they'll feel butterflies in their stomach when they're going through the highs and lows of your success and failure. True advocates may come in many forms, from those who'll trust you, believe in you and have faith you'll deliver to those who'll bleed for you. But true advocates they must be, rather than people who've simply stated that they're fans.

Which means they expect things from you. They don't expect you to be passive and simply go about your business. They don't expect you to ignore them when they raise a pressing, prominent or significant new issue with you. They don't expect to be treated disrespectfully, even though they know that ultimately they're expected to spend money with you and endorse you to others. They don't expect for you to grow out of touch with their wants and needs, so that they no longer feel you're relevant to them or have grown complacent on the back of success that they've helped to engineer.

But they do expect their role in your fortunes to be acknowledged. They do expect you to understand their frustrations, hopes, fears, excitement and at least some of the reasons why they support you. They do expect to be afforded some courtesy, although in the main they understand, or hopefully do, that they can only be afforded a little courtesy, because there are lots of other people who expect the same. They do expect you to understand at least a little about them, and if you meet that desire for some engagement with a showing of mutual desire, then the potential for trust, belief and eventually faith is laid out before you.

Because, really, it's a relationship and brands have to invest time, effort and money in sustaining relationships with an awful lot of people. The investment is necessary, and if well applied can go a long, long way.

At the heart of that shield, then, needs to be a core of trust, driven by a detailed understanding of the audience. And like parenting, understanding is something that has to be worked at, and gaining it is a never-ending challenge. Again, like parenting, trust is not something that can be bought, nor is it a consequence of the comfort of familiarity over time. It has to be earned.

Trust is truly the foundation stone of a brand's ability to shield itself against the worst effects of brand vandalism. If the brand is fundamentally trusted by the people it most wants to engage as its audience, it is far more difficult for detractors to damage its reputation. That is, of course, unless it decided to do something utterly stupid or is the unfortunate and accidental victim of something that detrimentally affects the way the audience feels about it. Nevertheless, with a high level of trust, the brand can enjoy a degree of insulation, providing that that trust is well placed, and anchored on acknowledged truth.

Beyond trust, though, there are the even more powerfully emotive forces of belief and faith. Once that core of trust has been not only established but maintained, and has perhaps overcome a series of challenges that could have derailed it, the brand's work in continuing to engage positively and empathetically with its audience gives it the best possible opportunity to nurture belief. It sounds simple, doesn't it? Surely brands that strive to speak clearly and truthfully will be believed? In a crowded, noisy world wracked with cynicism and in which trust has often been abused, audiences can be forgiven for not always believing what they hear. So sustained belief is, like trust, a privilege that must be earned, and takes time.

Believable – and believed – brands are in a strong position

reputationally. Providing the claims of detractors aren't true, they have a deflector shield that will be the envy of others. What they say, typically, is what the audience will believe, will talk about and is what has the potential to turn any act of deliberate reputation sabotage into a positive. Because the audience believes the brand is above all that.

And when that belief is sustained and polished, and its causes – its purposes – are things that have deep, emotive meaning for people's lives, belief can cross over into faith. Functional faith at first perhaps, but the pinnacle may be unequivocal, unbending faith.

We can but hope.

It would mean a shield of belief. Like a religion, without the religious fervour, but with a certain kind of fervour about and around the brand that acts as an insulation against attacks. The audience may actually come to disbelieve the claims of detractors. The defences of the brand's hard-earned reputation are actually raised far higher as a result of the strength of feeling in its favour. That shield will never be impenetrable, and its strength can be quickly lost unless it's properly maintained. And its shape and size must be adjusted continually as the threat from the enemy changes.

But a shield can be maintained. It can be an effective, comprehensive and thoroughly well deserved defence mechanism. But it will always remain perhaps only seconds from being totally undermined, if failure to tell the truth, attempts to conceal a lie or contemptuous disrespect for the audience come to the fore. Such situations are highly likely to become public – and if they're not, you're living on your wits, and surviving on luck.

What you do, not what you say

There are many ways to make constructive, sustainable efforts to replace luck with certainty. The daddy of them all, and rightly so in the post-spin age, is behaviour. Because what the brand does, not what it says, should have the greatest impact on its reputation and the in-built assets it will have to counter brand vandalism.

Brands belong to the audience, not to the organisation that produces the goods or services with which the brands are associated. They're complex entities built up in layers, often over years, and the distant memories of audiences can have as much effect as those affected by the most recent piece of communications.

And they're the things that saboteurs prize most highly. Because the organisations they're targeting don't and can't ultimately control their brands, so they can go after the hearts and minds of their audiences. They can try to sway them. And with modern media, those attacks can be more swift and more deadly. If the organisations behind the brands have acted in a sustained, unethical fashion according to accepted values, have been dishonest or have done something illegal, then unless there are exceptional circumstances they deserve all that they get from detractors. But if not, and the attacks are spurious or malicious, then brands need to ensure their defences are raised by centring the efforts of the softer underbelly that brand vandals will seek to strike at first: their behaviour.

So what is behaviour? Here's a definition: behaviour is the range of actions and mannerisms made by organisms, systems or artificial entities in conjunction with their environment, which includes the other systems or organisms around as well as the physical environment. Complicated, eh?

Well let's try a more simplistic take on it. Brands are controlled by the perceptions of people, and for people, behaviour can be common, unusual, acceptable or unacceptable. At a time when supposed gurus are charging handsome fees and waxing lyrical about the magic and the majesty of brand experiences, those concerned with reputation are going to great lengths to point out that experiences are fleeting, whereas the deep-rooted basis on which the organisation functions and its sustained investments in playing its part as a positive corporate citizen will have a greater lasting effect on brand perception, and so improve its defences. It's not only a central pillar of consumers' decisions to put one brand over another; it's the bricks on which reputational defences can be built.

And it's about substantial, specific and quantifiable changes, unless the brand already happens to have chosen a path of positive or even exemplary behaviour. It's no longer enough just to do it; to protect the brand you've got to show consistently how and that you're doing it. And tell stories around why you're doing it.

Behaviour can't just be token gestures propped up by marketing, though. It can't only be authentic, it has to be genuine. It has to come from within, which typically means a willingness to change.

It's also not just about you (nor is your brand). You cannot have a behaviour plan. To that extent brand behaviour is much like the behaviours of individual human beings, and their perceptions and reputations are determined by many of the same factors. Have too much of an ego and you'll come a cropper, unless you admit it publicly. Be rude to others and people who witness it will probably think badly of you. Lie and you'll be shunned if you're found out. Unless you're respected and trusted, people may listen but they won't believe or have genuine faith in you. If you're acting in good faith with good intentions, with the interests of others at heart as well as your own, and if you're prepared to play fair as well as use your assets to get ahead, there's a good chance your natural behaviour will become an advantage for you. If you act like a cock and are seen as a cock, it's probably because you are a cock.

Behaviour needs to be sustained too though and that's where human beings can fall down. It takes a lot of effort to keep maintaining reputation by showing positive behaviour, but it's an awful lot easier if that behaviour is natural and intrinsic rather than packaged and manufactured. And if it's the latter, people will see through that anyway.

The point here is that consistency is a virtue. Behaviour must be a commitment that's implemented persistently, no matter what. It must be part of the organisation's DNA, or the air that it breathes. It cannot be an initiative, a campaign or a project; it must be something that is orchestrated, nurtured and carefully fostered from the top down, and exemplified in the important things that everyone does. And communications must show that behaviour on the inside is demonstrated on the outside consistently, unwaveringly and potently. Given the fact that the walls between audience groups have come down, that should just happen naturally anyway, shouldn't it?

No more dirty little secrets?

The rotten core of many an intended unblemished behavioural record is that thing that tends to be the biggest blotter of the reputational copybook, because its revelation and its impact can rarely be foreseen. It is the dirty little secret. And dirty little secrets can quickly become big dirty stains.

That core is more visible than ever because of media change, and the era of transparent and agile business that it has prompted. That means that secrets are far harder to keep in the digital age because of the very reason that makes digital media so powerful – it's absolutely direct and it leaves an audit trail.

Will stuff really get found out, though? Well, quite simply, yes it probably will. Maybe not immediately, maybe not for a very long time, but probably eventually. And the more media change forces transparency, the greater the reputational harm those naughty secrets may cause when they eventually come out. The more you're seen to have hidden or obscured the truth, or turned a blind eye to a process that could have revealed it, the more you'll be held to account and the more animated the criticism or negative feeling is likely to be. There is also a social climate amongst many audiences that's founded on a consensus that times have changed because of media evolution, and so there's nothing whatsoever to gain and an awful lot to lose from keeping it behind closed doors. A cover-up is never clever, but nor will it be forgiven, unless it's absolutely exceptional.

Should organisations be expected to tell the whole truth and nothing but the truth, then? Contentious point maybe, but our belief is no. They can't be, because some things are confidential or there is a need to protect individuals or society at large by not revealing them. Providing that it's for the right reasons, of course. In fact in many cases it may be commercially unwise or just plain unnecessary to give a full and frank account – but it does need to be frank. The point is that it must be fundamentally honest, without attempting to conceal or dishonestly water down untruths.

There should always be some secrets. It wouldn't be competitive business or a dutiful public organisation without them would it? But the information that is kept confidential must not be deliberately concealed because of fears of reprisals, personal repercussions or legal action, but because it is fair, just or appropriate – according to the law or socially accepted norms – that it remains under lock and key. There is a distinction between secrets and information that must or should remain confidential, and most rational members of the audience understand that.

The important thing is for organisations to consider doing an audit of sensitive information within their walls, assessing everything and working out whether or not the information is being treated appropriately. In the past, there could be any element of hope that bad things wouldn't be found out. Most of this should already have been laid out on the table by compliance and legal teams, but skeletons will always exist. In planning the best reputational defences available, it's best to get it all out in the open internally, so decisions can be made about whether to get it all out in the open externally.

Transparency, then, is at a premium. Modern media forces it, although it has long been received wisdom anyway. But in providing the ability to look inside, you'd better make sure that what's on display is the truth, and presented in the way you want it to be seen. Received wisdom of brands choosing to live behind a virtual wall and only choosing to communicate externally on their own terms, largely as and when it suited them, rather than being just a click away from external audiences, has been turned on its head. That relatively artificial operating environment, in which brands could, if they wanted to, knowingly conceal information has gone.

In its place is a communications landscape that means it may well be better to opt to share information publicly that previously would have remained very much behind closed doors. The risk of reputational damage – or other direct financial harm, such as from legal action – can be substantial. Not just to behave ethically and adhere to high professional codes of conduct, but to go further in sharing more information on what's going on inside the organisation or what its future plans are than would have ever been shared in years gone by. As media change and the audience-led appetite for fairness and cleanliness have forced a requirement for greater – and in some cases near-total – transparency, so has that transparency agenda prompted a rethink on clarity. Rather than just being clear when it suits, then, brands are realising that clarity is not just something to approach with caution, but something that can be turned into a tangible reputational asset.

Just like periods of extreme bad news – the stock market wobble after the dotcom flop, or the aftermath of the public admission that the credit crunch had taken its grip – brands are also learning that it's sometimes okay to air your dirty linen in public. Get it out of the way, take the hit on reputation as others around you are suffering the same ignominy, and you'll fare better than having to confess you have bad news when the rest of the market is smelling of roses.

The managed dissemination of bad stuff is better than the unmanaged dissemination of bad stuff. Particularly when someone else who doesn't like you is calling the shots. It does mean that brands have to become comfortable with something that many of them would never have entertained in the past: the communication of negative or neutral information, and even presenting positive information without the fat layer of lip gloss that they may have applied in the past. While only a few brave brands had the foresight to do this before the rise of the Internet and social media, the pragmatism attached to such honest self-assessment can go a long way to build a trustworthy and believable reputation today. And one in which those in the audience who are passionate about the brand and the business behind it can have practically unwavering faith.

The Greenpeace evolution

Greenpeace is perhaps the archetypcal campaigning organisation, taking brands and governments to task on environmental and ethical issues for decades. It has been progressively modernising its approach to campaigning with the rise of digital media and shows a clear innovative streak in its latest work.

The view of Nic Seton, digital campaigner for Greenpeace, is that the Internet has both empowered the organisation and levelled the playing field.

'Society currently operates in a democratic deficit that facilitates corporate profiteering over social, environmental and economic concerns, as well as citizen disenfranchisement. Low-cost, distributed communications technology is the greatest threat available to that mode,' he told the authors in research for the book.

Greenpeace appreciates that it is addressing a wise audience, one sensitive to hypocrisy and that is setting the rules of the 'game'. It also believes the Internet has had an additive effect on its communications: conversation as well as broadcast information, relationships as well as radicalism, adaptation as well as innovation. In what Greenpeace calls a renaissance in international social organisation, it sets out five audience expectations that help shape its campaigns:

- Be social, not rude or anti-corporate
- Inspire people through storytelling
- Bad relations spoil the party
- Demonstrate interdependence
- Fail fast and be humble

You'll never talk alone

Well there's a sub-heading that will bring a smile to the face of every Liverpool FC fan, and a wince to the face of all others. There's a weak but somewhat relevant parallel here, though. Football (it's known as soccer in some parts of the world) teams can enjoy unfalteringly passionate support from their fans, meaning that with an army of followers on their side, the spirit of teams can be lifted on the pitch and prompt them to greater achievements. The factor that tends to give a slight advantage to the home team is always those tens of thousands of committed fans cheering their team on.

And while they may cheer in silence, smart brands can seek a similar kind of backing from their advocates and biggest fans, and it can help carry them through tough times. But unlike most football clubs, this does centre on a level of sustained actual engagement from the audience – and it means brand communications becomes much less about command and control, and much more about command and entrust.

Because if you want your audience to trust you, and engagement is at the heart of the relationship with the brand, then you're going to have to trust them, too.

So there is no control, but there never was anyway: brands that tried to control their messages in the days of one-way media often strived for as much control as possible over how journalists and editors relayed their information, but it was ultimately out of their hands. In these days of two-way media, a highly engaged audience that trusts the brand and can be trusted to help defend it against attacks is an enviable shield. It can protect a brand when reputation battles are fought with external detractors.

Brands don't exist in a vacuum. They exist in the hearts and minds of the audience, and while corporations may do their utmost to shape them, brands live or die by what audiences think or feel about them. But those same people are subjected to the attentions of thousands if not millions of other brands too, and the discussions that go on around and about brands do not happen in isolation. Reputational attacks are by their very nature carried out in the most public forums possible, but that means that they too can be scrutinised and commented on by the people in the brand's audience who the detractors are trying to convince. The transparency and democracy of the Internet mean that there's nowhere to hide, but there's also no way of laying dirty tricks behind someone's back, either. Ultimately, no matter how innovative and incisive the techniques used to communicate, the people will decide. And rightly so.

Put this way, the Internet looks like a very fair environment in which to communicate. It may be, but it's also open season for vandals wanting to take a shot at brands, or formulate a sustained onslaught. Beyond that, though, where fairness matters most is whether the brand behaves ethically, legally and fairly, and is a good citizen in going about its business. If it is, it should always have way more friends than enemies. It if isn't, and it can only muster a small band of paid mercenaries to try to protect it from a braying mob around the world, then an impartial observer might call that justice.

Many brands lie somewhere in between those two positions; not completely holy, and with some practices being hangovers from an age when less ethical business practices were acceptable. Or perhaps some practices that are commonplace in some sectors are frowned upon in others. There may be skeletons in the closet from something the brand did a long time ago. Equally, it could have nothing but positive intentions and business practices but failed to have explained them well externally.

Every brand is different and there is no one-size-fits-all solution to getting a brand on the front foot reputationally. But it is always worth examining what reputational threats already exist, from current or past business activities, and having a detailed plan to either change the way of working or take positive steps to repair the damage of yesteryear. It takes patience, diligence, and a lot of hard work. Above all it takes a deep and sustained understanding of the audience, through effective engagement.

An audience that has latched on to such a brand can give it

the most effective shield it can ever hope for: the protection of the crowd, the very people who brand vandals are aiming to reach in their bid to wreak havoc. When attacks happen, those people need to stand up for the brand and they're much more likely to do so if they not only feel like they're engaged with the brand but that it's listening to them, talking back and even enabling the most vitriolic supporters to participate in some way in its activities and future plans.

One of the most important reasons why the audience can be so effective as a defence mechanism is that no matter how well trusted the brand is, the audience is always likely to be more trusted because of its supposed impartiality. It's one of the core tenets of public relations, and it's something that brands would do well to remember as they seek to engage audiences not just to make it easier for them to sell products or services, but to gain the loyalty and support of the people who value them the most for reputational protection purposes.

Brands have to earn the trust of their audience and then trust their audience to protect them. It may be a concept that would have been scoffed at in the days before the Internet, but the best brands are the ones that stand together with their audiences, and work with them to further develop that understanding into deep-rooted belief and faith in the brand's intentions. Providing that position is never abused, it's a lofty one that makes attacks on the brand more difficult to orchestrate, easier to spot and probably far less successful. Where there is a sustained relationship based on genuine dialogue, reputation can gain a lustre that is very difficult for anyone to tarnish. There may be a saying that mud sticks, but it's much more difficult to adhere to a highly polished shield.

CHAPTER 9

BULLETS TO BROWNIE POINTS

Brand vandals expect to prey on fear. Don't fuel it for them.
#BrandVandals

It's said the best form of defence is offence. But that's much easier said than done in a lot of situations.

Having made all the right moves and exhibited persistent due diligence in order to build an effective shield against reputational attacks, any organisation can be forgiven for wanting to go a step further and trying to figure out how it might be able to turn vandalism to its advantage.

Again, though, that's easier said than done.

Before we look at that, let's look at why a brand might want to do this at a commercial level. It's often said that board and senior management teams typically don't fully understand the value of communications, so why might they be interested in how to turn the bleakest of reputation wallopings into some big perception gains, beyond the obvious reversal of potential financial loss?

What is the board really looking for?

It's fairly obvious what the board will really be looking for, given its remit: managed and sustained financial success while fulfilling its promises as an organisation in doing so. The question is where reputation and deliberate attempts to spoil it cut across that.

The obvious big factor here is risk. The risk that comes with poor or sullied reputation is an enormous one, and it's this risk that the board ultimately wants to cut down to size, and indeed turn into a certainty by transforming a bad situation into a good one; by not just deflecting the bullets, but by catching them, turning them back on the enemy and so earning lots of brownie points from the audience in the process. (A brownie, by the way, is an English organisation for young girls who, amongst other things, earn points for good behaviour and doing good deeds. Hence the saying.)

Risk management is front and centre of what the board is seeking. It wants to know that whatever the attempt to derail the brand's reputation through deliberate sabotage, the risk has been assessed and the threats can be assessed, tackled and hopefully nullified. From a scary situation that it has little direct capability to counter, the board is looking for some sort of certain outcome.

In order to be certain, it first wants to be clear on the extent and the nature of the risk it faces. Which is tough when you don't truly understand the ins and outs of it, and rely on communications experts to quantify things and map a path of action through the mud that has been slung. But those two – clarity and certainty – go hand in hand. First the board needs to be clear on the risks it faces and the risks associated with trying to overcome the situation, and then it needs to ascertain what it can be certain of, and what remains a risk.

That's most likely all the board is looking for. It all makes common sense, it's all good business practice and they're the obvious priorities. What the board could, and probably should, be looking for, though, is something that can empower it to make more assertive and more impactful decisions in the wake of such a communications crises. It should be looking for a response plan that makes its reactive communications, issued in response to the challenge, gel with or even embellish the regular communications work it's doing to build the reputation of the brand.

It should be looking for the response to strike a chord with the audience by pinpointing the one thing about the brand that enables it to stand apart, that has the potency to drive commercial value and is what all of its communications should hinge on.

Its difference.

Because while a brand that exudes true difference is a more powerful brand and one that is more likely to drive sales, a reputation that is driven by corporate behaviour but intersects and is therefore bolstered by brand perception is a very difficult thing to dislodge. Its strength not only has tangible commercial value, but gives it muscle.

And is it really possible to turn a negative into a positive?

This section could be summed up with one short sentence: Use the truth to stop a snowball from building, then lob it back at them.

But before we get cosy with the truth, let's look at the one biggest, yet most unfair, reason why a reputation can be left battered and tattered in a matter of minutes – all because someone lies about you.

Truth is, of course, what matters above all else in determining how best to handle any situation where an act of brand vandalism has been or is being committed. If what someone is saying about your brand is fundamentally untrue, you are in the strongest possible position to deal with the incident. A public statement stating what is untrue, why it's untrue and – if you feel the situation merits it – a perspective on what your opinion is on the lie having been published, is the very least the brand should be doing to put right the inaccuracy. And it needs to happen at the earliest available opportunity after the lie has been communicated.

More often than not, there will also be some sort of response.

It could be an insistence that the offending party apologises. It could be that there is some form of action taken to ensure that the offender is banned from making such statements again. More likely, you'll be working with the authorities to seek prosecution as a criminal or civil offence will have been committed, with the effort invested in finding the culprit no doubt proportionate to the scale of damage that could have been – or was – caused, the nature of the matter in hand and whether other unrelated incidents are also alleged to have been the work of the same party.

That's the clear-cut stuff, though. Shades of grey may mean that while an offending statement may not be untrue in its entirety, some of it is. Which forces a tough decision: do you go public to right the wrong knowing that doing so will draw perhaps unwelcome attention to the part of the content that isn't technically a lie? Each situation will have to be assessed on its own merits or drawbacks. Similarly, when something contains no untruth but the content appears to have been deliberately engineered to be misleading, the act of clarifying things can open up a whole can of worms that you'd rather keep the lid on.

The bottom line is it pays to tell the truth, provide context and be transparent about the things that matter most, even if you're not legally obliged to. And if the brand may not always have done that in the past, it had better be prepared to justify the reason why.

Another consideration, and one that may not be through a deliberate attempt to trash the brand or is at best an extremely amateur one, is that the attack may come in the form of confused or misguided gossip. It may just been someone starting a rumour, making an irreverent remark or drawing a far-fetched conclusion against their better judgement. What then? Well there are common policies for crisis management situations about not being drawn into commenting on rumours or speculation – every media training course worth its salt will tell you that. But the important thing is not to take the bait: whereas mistakes or idle speculation may be quashed or otherwise countered swiftly and clinically, if the person or group stirring it up is provoking the brand by using gossip as an alternative weapon to issuing an incorrect statement or other piece of communications about you, in the hope that you'll be duped into confirming it, don't fall for it. Not only will you probably regret it commercially, but you'll have to suffer the indignity of some scheister having put one over on you.

Let's look at scenarios where attacks can be turned around, and work to the assumption that the act of sabotage against the brand is either fundamentally untrue or is defensible in the view of the majority of the brand's audience. In other words, it will be good for your reputation to go public. Well, in that case the most important thing to think about is the people who should be at the epicentre of your actions: your audience. As we've already discussed, having engaged your audience so that those people trust the brand, and have belief or even faith in what you provide to them, you'll have mobilised an army that will help to shield your reputation. In turning around a bad situation into one that should benefit your reputation, knowing or being able to reasonably preempt how your audience will react to your actions is the most crucial consideration of all. You don't just have to know who your friends are, you have to know what they'll think and what they'll do. And if your data and judgement are right, they'll have your back.

That's particularly important when you consider how the appetite for scrutiny of such apparent transgressions – in other words, there now tends to be feeding frenzies across all types of media around untruths until they're proven to be unfounded – has increased since media began fragmenting and digitising. In the time before the Internet, or more specifically before the Web became a publishing platform, journalists were the main force in investigating what brands may have done wrong or where the organisations behind them may have acted improperly. Since media began digitising, journalists have been going far, far beyond that. They used to simply interview whistle-blowers in the event of a potential scandal, whereas now the extent to which they raise spectres and cause fingers to be pointed can pour lighter fluid on situations that are already combustible. One article or one blog post is no longer something that is assessed by other media the next day or before the next available editions, and may be the source of follow-up pieces. Today, the number of editorial pieces on a breaking story can mushroom into dozens within minutes, be tweeted and retweeted, parodied on YouTube, Flickr, Instagram and through Vines.

Stopping that snowball from turning into an avalanche has become one of the most strenuous and most sought-after skills in communications. There is no silver bullet for turning bad publicity into good, but a measured response that assesses the scale and nature of the negative exposure, and is backed up with accurate data and verifiable facts, tends to be the cornerstone. It can hold the key to redemption.

First, though, the brand has to consider whether it has made mistakes, and if so must admit and correct them. If it's in the wrong, it can only turn reputation around if its moves into the right. Think about the major product recall scandals of recent years that started as a few real conversations, then moved into social media and were inflamed when they were picked up by the regular press. It may even mean making drastic changes to operations as well as a quick fix to a product or service, but unless that action is swift then the brand's work to turn the story around into a tale of how it is acting responsibly in making amends can soon become shrouded in more controversy, because the bid to make things good becomes a story in its own right.

Finally, it's important to remember that one thing is unobtainable in all of this – perfection. There is no such thing as a perfect plan or perfect response to a brand attack. One hundred marks out of one hundred is a ridiculous dream to chase. But with some care, some cohesion and some cunning, some top marks can be scored.

Engaging the staff to bolster the fans

We've already looked at the value of engaged audiences in providing a shield against attacks. One audience group that should be considered a special case, but that it can be easy to overlook in a panic, is the brand's own people. Staff are crucial, because reputational gains begin at home.

They are also a key part of ensuring that trust, belief and faith in the brand can be restored quickly or can avoid being lost in the first place, because if the staff aren't on board and openly supporting the brand at a time of attack, the organisation is not only weaker but compromised. If staff don't only exhibit belief but decry the action against the brand, it's easy to see why the external audience may start to doubt the allegations that have been made. Like watching two opponents arguing in the street or two boxers sparring in the ring, attention will quickly flit from one party to the other, and the brand and its people need to be unwavering. Given the number of people who work for a brand who are likely to be engaged in social networks these days, it is impossible to issue blanket bans on all external communications to anyone other than authorised spokespeople only. Instead, staff that have influential social media connections should be mobilised to support the brand, rather than forced to hide in the shadows.

Priming staff to act that way depends on many factors, not

least the way the organisation treats its people generally. It's important to ensure that there is persistent, open dialogue between the organisation or brand and the people who work for it. Not just the one-dimensional and one-directional methods of internal communications that most organisations used in years gone by, but sustained two-way communication, with staff engaged digitally alongside customers, partners and stakeholders, as an equally important audience.

Open dialogue, then, is crucial. So is courtesy, and one of the best ways to ensure there is a strong level of trust with staff at the time of a brand attack it is to turn to them first, or at the same time as external communications swings into action. Don't just assume staff will pick up on everything anyway and that the priority lies outside the organisation – instead, demonstrate that the brand trusts them by involving them from the off. The communications team will need to move at lightning speed anyway, so you may as we'll set things up so that they have sufficient resources to engage the internal audience too. You're going to need them, regardless of the role they play in stemming the flow of blood or turning tables on the opposition.

Better still, as part of the ongoing work to build and sustain the brand's reputation, those internal advocates should ideally already be engaged as ambassadors. Rather than a sleeping army waiting to be called into action, it would be better if as many of them as possible were already imparting some level of influence amongst external audiences on behalf of the brand, however casual a form that may take. The more their word can be taken seriously and believed, the less spring-into-action communications will be heavily scrutinised in case it is an obvious example of the brand having called them in and put words into their mouths.

Not just the executives at the top and the communications

team, either, but everyone in the business whose role and personality command a strong and engaged following; the kind of people with no incentive to bend the truth and who are there-fore ideal candidates for pulling doubters on-side in the case of a reputation attack. Depending on the brand of course, the likes of scientists and engineers, technologists, analysts, accountants and support staff are the people whose words can carry more weight than those who are normally thrust into the spotlight to speak up.

They are the people who are likely to be more trusted, and there should be no qualms about encouraging them to stand up for the brand in times of trouble. Indeed, the entire internal audience is more likely to be trusted than the brand itself, which only exists in the hearts and minds of the audience anyway. Any of the simple rules apply – give them some content, even if it's just a statement, and encourage them to share it on social networks with a comment. In fact, do this right and you probably won't even need to encourage them or give any instructions on what to do – they'll know what to do anyway. And that will make it natural, which stands to make the communications more powerful and more authentic.

This democratic approach to communications and the abil-ity for a brand to appear confident and in control when countering the attack, rather than panicked and doubtful while it scrambles for statements, is a crucial asset. In the age of one-way media, and something that's still a common prac-tice for tabloid newspapers, journalists would seek to hunt down a 'source' inside the brand who they could convince to give a close-up perspective on a situation, even though such techniques usually relied on scant information or things being 'confirmed' only because the source failed to deny them or no evidence was presented to the contrary. This all happens because there is a natural and often feverish curiosity about what's actually going on inside the brand, and because journalists would otherwise have no way to make their story stand up. It turns the source into a mystery figure, to the extent that many brands failed to ever trace who it was who squealed, if indeed the quotes were genuine.

But by turning the inside to the outside, there's next to no risk that media of any kind will have to go looking for a source. And if they did, that perspective would be drowned out by the volume and authenticity of comment and content from other staff within the organisation. It's not about letting your own people take the bullets, it's about them helping to drive the brownie points in your direction.

Mobilising commercial engagement: partners

It's a similar story outside the business if you consider what your partners might be able to do to support your cause. Those partners might be product development businesses, suppliers or retail channels. It doesn't really matter; the important point is that they have a direct line into your audience, and in some cases see them face to face around the clock.

Imagine you're responsible for communications at a food brand that is subject to an act of brand vandalism about methods you employ in your supply chain in other countries, with the finger pointing firmly at your animal welfare record in Southern Europe. The brand vandals launch their onslaught by hacking your Facebook page, turning your brand characters there into disease-ridden pigs, their bodies emblazoned with allegations of how poor your record of transporting animals for slaughter is.

But it's not true. So you remove the offending page quickly, state the facts via a short video from your CEO, issue that on social networks and point enquiring journalists to it. Your staff are briefed to view it and are able to share it. A well-oiled communications process is rolled out internally and externally.

Two hours later, a customer approaches the tills at a supermarket with one of your products in hand. He says to the till operator, 'Hang on, isn't this one of those sausages made out of the pigs with disease?'

'Yeah, it might be,' says the spotty till operator. 'I read something about that, I think.'

That's how rumours can spread, and how an otherwise-watertight communications process can seep at the seams. And that's just a small example.

Partners are an important bunch to remember. They're pseudo-spokespeople and they can quickly point to a misalignment between how the brand is responding and reality, even if that misalignment is a fallacy. And the thing is, they have a vested interest in helping, because their success is partly tied to yours, and so if your brand suffers, so will their business, and potentially their brand, too. Like your staff, it would be best if they stood firm with you, as the more visibility for your counter-attack the better.

There are practical considerations to this, too, as your partners' audiences may extend further than your own audience. Taking the food brand example, your core audience is likely to be the people who buy and eat your product regularly or fairly regularly. But retailers of that product will have many other customers and other audiences who don't eat your food regularly or at all, and those people can have a degree of influence over your core audience. They can start to sway the minds of your core customers – but conversely, if they, the people who don't eat your product, aren't convinced by what the brand vandals have been trying to put in their minds, and they share their views with your customers, they're likely to be seen as legitimate and trustworthy.

So your partners are important, and their ability to increase the reach of your message and in doing so provide an extra level of influence over your audience makes them even more important.

How leaders must bring this all together

When reputational attacks move beyond the brand or product, when people must front the effort to put the record straight and even reach a higher standing in the minds of the audience, there's no denying who's most in the firing line. It's time for the leaders to stand up and be counted.

They know this. There's nowhere to hide. It's a situation that very few of them will relish. Yet they're crucial to how reputation rebounds or strengthens. And it starts long before the poo comes into contact with the rotating air movement device.

This is all about behaviour, pure and simple. Because behaviour has the biggest impact on how a brand is perceived, and the behaviour of leaders has a cumulative yet incisive bearing on perception and reputation.

There is no alternative, then, other than for leaders to be upstanding role models for their brands at all times. That doesn't mean not being themselves, but it does mean behaving in line with the brand's ethical stance, compassionately, legally, in accordance with the brand's values and above all genuinely at all times. You'd think that's the least a brand should expect from its leaders, yet it hasn't always been the case. Brands make promises, and these days more than ever before, their leaders have to – and have to be seen to – keep those promises through the way that they behave.

Behaviour will also have the biggest overall impact on how damage is not just minimised but repaired and turned into a positive. The way that leaders behave in responding to brand attacks not only singles out their leadership qualities but puts any deficiencies under the most brilliant of spotlights. They must be seen to act quickly, responsibly, fairly, decisively, ethically, morally and with utmost commitment to upholding the truth. That wouldn't be a bad checklist for a day at the office, would it?

And that's just to get them to breakeven, and stand a chance of plugging the reputational gaps. To get on the front foot, deflect or take a stranglehold on what vandals have claimed about the brand and turn it into a win, they've got to consider what type of behaviour must be exuded in order to develop that kind of belief in their audience. We're talking about things like valour, ingenuity, empathy, cunning, guile and flair. The things that can instantly gain a high level of respect because they trigger a deep-rooted emotional reaction.

And often, they can be things that, providing it's appropriate, can make the audience smile. If the allegations or criticism are unfounded and ludicrous to the point of being funny, then why not turn the tables by using humour to counter them? It will certainly make your communications memorable, and go a long way to rekindling or safeguarding respect. Brands should also remember that while a reputational attack may be far from funny when they're in the eye of that particular storm, for their competitors and peers in other industries, there may be brownie points in them making you the butt of the joke. Again, far better to take command of that situation by leading the conversation or the joke than trying to make light of it later when you're surrounded by the noise of laughter.

To do that, leaders must be inherently communicative. They must do all they can to ensure that when the moment comes for them to step into the breach and defend the brand, they're as comfortable as they can be with it and are already seen as the familiar face of the brand, rather than a leader who is rarely seen in the public gaze. It's fairly simple: if people know who you are and already have a degree of respect for you, they're fare more likely to listen. They'll be more willing to see the attack as something against you personally, and so far more ready have empathy with or sympathy for you. Of course, your detractors could have a charismatic frontman who stands up and points the finger, but given the nature of co-ordinated reputation attacks these days that's fairly unlikely. More often than not, they'll be faceless.

Being familiar means being omnipresent in the owned content that the brand controls, seen regularly in the conventional press, and being prominent and influential on social networks. Getting the leader to appear in your owned content should be fairly straightforward; it's a question of diary management and a good briefing. Conventional media profiling relies on sound editorial content planning, potent messaging, opportunistic agility in pursuing new routes to publicity and just being damned persistent in chasing ink – or, more likely, pixels.

Social networks are trickier because the leader has to have a sustained personal commitment and interest in engaging with the audience. Does that just mean that some leaders will be better than others at doing this, that some will know instinctively what to do whereas others will need handholding every step of the way? Yes, partly, but in the future the continued fragmentation and intimacy of media may make socially engaged leaders a prerequisite, rather than a benefit. In the future, it may well be a legitimate question to ask how a leader, who must guide a brand and make it attractive to its audience and fulfil commercial goals can be effective if he or she is not directly and powerfully engaged with that audience. Be honest, you can see it coming, can't you?

Like brands themselves, leaders really have to be engaged these days – or make a powerful virtue of their aloofness. When attacks happen, brands really want their most influential core audience to turn to brand leaders for their wisdom, their insight, their perspective and most of all for their assurance that it isn't true. CEOs must not only be engaging, they must be engaged. In a different way to brands, perhaps, but typically with the same audiences, and with a clarity and a willingness to lead conversations and interject in others, so that when a crisis breaks, the audience is poised and ready to hang on their every word, rather than standing well back and wondering what the brand might do in response.

Leaders can also make a big difference in their insistence on brands being ready for attack, and in doing so invest time, resources and emotion in things that will be an asset in the midst of an onslaught. Perhaps the single biggest thing they can do operationally within the organisation is to drive insistence that the brand does everything it can to understand its audience. No guessing, no assumption, no hope, just a whole heap of data that's refreshed constantly and pored over in detail. It needs to assess context as well as patterns. It needs to identify influencers, how they're connected, how their views might change, who they have influence over and what about.

Most importantly, audience insight needs to give the brand the power to be able to second-guess accurately how people will react to certain situations and know the brand's planned reaction to them. We've used the word 'guess' there deliberately because ultimately that's what it will be: there are no certainties when it comes to defending reputations against attacks like these, only extremely likely outcomes based on expertise, understanding and the sophisticated engineering of communications. There will always be an element of guesswork but the more audience data the brand has and the better it has scrutinised it, the better chance it will stand. The risk of misreading the audience will have been virtually eliminated.

That understanding has to extend beyond the brand. It can't

just look at attitude towards a brand or its products, or that brand category, or the brand's leaders, or its heritage; indeed it needs to go completely off-piste. It needs to examine the entire ecosystem of the business and its activities, as well as the macro issues of the markets in which the brand operates, the global socio-economic climate and its applicability on a hyperlocal level and the primary wants, needs and fears of the target audience. Not much, then.

It is an enormous mountain of data, some of it structured but much of it dynamic. Amassing it is daunting, and keeping on top if it requires a sharp eye and dogged determination. But in all likelihood, similar levels of diligence, endeavour and scrutiny are being employed elsewhere in the organisation as part of ongoing operations. The lens just needs to be turned on data that impacts reputation and reputation planning. And it is ultimately the job of leaders to make sure that happens. They and they alone can make audience understanding one of the biggest commercial priorities.

Leaders can also have a cultural impact on the organisation that will affect its readiness and adeptness to take charge and turn an attack into a gain. The most prominent area in which their influence can be felt is a very functional and none-too-interesting one, but it is vital. They need to ensure a process of constant improvement in behaviour and communication. Some of that can come from instinct, some from hunches, but it must be underpinned by process, too. In this way, elements of inappropriate behaviour can be changed, the drive for appropriate behaviour can remain constant and all communications around crises, crucial areas of company policy or brand engagement around sensitive or emotive issues can be measured, understood, learned from and applied to improve processes for the future.

Above all, though, the role of a leader in turning bullet points into brownie points, by not only defending but enhancing reputation, simply centres on just doing the things that leaders do, and in ways that put reputation first. And at the heart of that is the way in which the decisions they make and actions they take have to ensure that the brand is highly engaged, that the audience is involved in its fortunes and understands its difference compared to competitors and that it is seen to stand strong in times of despair. By acting appropriately and pursuing a shrewd course of action, leaders can actually do some good to the reputation, rather than just being forced to defend it when it's suffering bruises.

Leaders' roles in driving engagement is to understand that media is a two-way phenomenon, and so plays a crucial role in brand perception, reputation and fortune. An engaged brand is on the path to communications being a commercial asset, whereas a disengaged brand is, these days, a drifter with pockets full of risk treading a long and lonely road. But while the ability to engage intermittently around campaigns can be driven by the marketing or communications department, the transition to engagement that is interlocked and sustained is something that must be backed or at least sanctioned by those at leadership level. They must not only understand the value of engagement for commercial outcomes but also for its defensive qualities when sabotage looms.

That drive can be hardened into an even greater asset, although it is tough to attain and even tougher to sustain: the active involvement of the most important members of the audience in the brand. Sure, marketing campaigns can achieve this, but having a central bank of influencers keyed and tuned in to the brand so much so that they effectively become part of its furniture requires gumption, skill and commitment that many brands can only aspire to. The best people to defend, uphold and strike down the detractors of the brand are the people who truly have cause to love it most – the people who spend money on it, and who cherish it emotionally. That means you have to let them in on it, and manage that experience so they don't just create a shield, but one that bullets will bounce off.

Finally, the thing that leaders must do in order to turn the bad into possible good is to be unwavering in the face of the storm. They must stand strong, confident that they are fully prepared not only to handle the snowballs that are coming their way, but to catch them and chuck them back with gusto. They must not buckle, or be afraid of the enemy.

This means thinking about a defence strategy well in advance, and that relies on them having an intimate appreciation of the value of reputation for their brand. In either direction.

Above all, they must lack fear, because that is the opposite of what brand vandals expect. They must be made of the sternest stuff, and have, as the Spanish might say, *más cojones*.

CHAPTER 10

FIT-FOR-PURPOSE COMMUNICATIONS

The qualities and skills of five-star communications teams, and how you can stand tall. #BrandVandals

It's only words and pictures, though, isn't it? If you compare what communications people do to people who actually put their lives on the line every day, they're hardly heroes, regardless of how clever they are at helping their brands to dodge the bullets.

In fact, what do communicators do all day, anyway? Make up stories? Sit around waiting for someone to say something, then figure out how to respond? Come up with shrewd, stunt-driven plans to get people talking about brands?

Well at a simplistic level, they do all of that. But in order to get a better understanding of what communications teams really do, it's probably worth looking first at what the rest of the organisation really *thinks* they do.

While this is hardly a statement that has been subject to any substantive research, it's pretty clear to anyone who has ever worked in a communications role that the vast majority of colleagues outside the team have next to no clue what communications people do all day. They can probably only imagine the tip of the iceberg of the work they actually do. That bit that they have been exposed to is probably, and quite naturally so, the most acute stuff that swings into action when really bad things happen. The statements made when the brand is enveloped in a crisis, or that are made when bad news is announced and taken on the chin, such as when the brand does something wrong, announces things that negatively affect personnel or suppliers, or has to explain itself in the case of a product recall.

Those are all crucial communications issues that can ultimately make or break a brand, its partnerships and the commitment of its people. They all need delicate handling. But they're only a tiny fraction of the work that goes on to plan, manage, deliver and analyse communications.

The scope of the communications team's role is far broader. Its job is to listen to what the audience is saying. Its job is to plan communications, both the speaking and the responding. Its job is to deliver conversation and to manage accusation. It is the brand's first and last line of defence. All of that takes a lot of planning, negotiating, authoring and measuring. Those words and pictures should never be chosen lightly.

When the brand's reputation is attacked, whether deliberately or because it has done something wrong or been found lacking, it's the communications team that has to engineer the response and assess what's in the brand's best interests for the long term. That's blindingly obvious from the contents of previous chapters, but it's worth reiterating that communicators are the ones in the firing line, even if it's the CEO who ultimately takes the rap. All eyes internally tend to fall on the communications team, and until relatively recently the way that responses to attacks happened were played out along common lines.

Firstly, there was the establishment of fact. Was what had been alleged actually true? If so, what was the nature of that truth, and what was behind it? What needed to, or could be, done to put the situation right, if anything? How many people externally knew about it, what would the likely consequences be and, crucially, how long would it be before the first media were able to assess and publicise the information?

Then came what needed to be said or explained in pictures, who needed to do that and what format it should all take. What would the likely response be? Had a crime been committed? What would the audience most likely think of all of this?

These are just some of the questions that are asked, but all of them share two main traits. Firstly, the remit of the communications team went way beyond just understanding communications and into gaining a firm grasp of the legal, commercial, moral and social ramifications of the situation. The audience's reaction had to be second-guessed and the 'statutory' obligations of the brand in society had to be clear. And secondly, they were all questions that typically gave communicators little time to think.

While crises like this are never nice to handle, at least communicators who'd gained some experience knew the rules and knew the ropes, so knew what to do – most of the time.

Immediacy has become the unseen enemy of the crisis response planner. The obvious difference is that there is now so little time to think of a plan of action and get materials together – where feasible, plans should have been drawn up well in advance and as much of the content as possible should already exist. There will always be new comment to provide for new situations, but if the brand already has a well-developed story, and is intent on truth and transparency, no surprise should be too big. And if the brand acts that way, even completely unforeseen surprises should be things it can take in its stride.

This means not so much a mass change of priorities for the communications team of today and one that is fit for the future, but one that has those priorities brought into very sharp focus. Most importantly, communications must be an active, engaged function rather than a passive one that relies purely on structured communications output, often through controllable channels.

For many brands, communications could be something they had to do, or that they chose to do through the prepared content of either a conventional press or regulated, self-published channels like newsletters and website content. Today the communications team has to operate in a persistent and all-embracing state of dialogue. Rather than popping into the room and choosing to say things when it best suits the brand, and perhaps turn a deaf ear without direct consequences, today it has to figure out how to be locked into conversations at all time – and not all of them welcome ones. It has to be in the room. It has to be prepared to be the centre of adoration, the centre of attention and the butt of jokes.

In many ways, brands today have to communicate like polite and sophisticated human beings do when they converse. Ever-listening, knowledgeable about the audience, ever-prepared to agree or disagree, pick up on a conversational thread, pay attention to and engage with those it dislikes, mindful of what may be going on in hushed tones or darkened corners.

I'm talking about proper, freshly prepared communications, rather than the tinned stuff that lurks in store cupboards and can be whipped out for an impromptu and poorly planned meal.

And possibly better than this book at metaphors.

Designed to be resilient?

But continuing in the same vein, the communications team of today has to be the mouth, eyes, ears and nose of the business, and of the brand. The communications environment in which the smart, progressive and well-defended brand has to prevail is pervasive and never stops. This was always really the case in days gone by, but the way brands were attacked used to be, well, more gentlemanly. There was time to think.

Like any creature facing unseen predators, brands need defending by communicators who cannot just see round corners, but can sense what's out there in the jungle and have an ear stuck to the ground for trouble. Because when trouble is approaching, it needs to be spotted early.

The ability to smell danger is the first factor to consider, but one that few brands have ever really had to consider in the past, unless they operated in particularly sensitive markets or had established enemies. Those enemies may not just have been competitors, either; they could have been legislators, partners, suppliers, perhaps governments, or even the emotionally unhinged. Today, on the Internet, they may just as easily be your own customers.

Smelling danger can only really be done by mapping the full environment in which the brand operates and should communicate. In today's global market, that can mean local markets, local workforces, competitors, laws, history, inherited issues through acquisitions and communities that have gathered on social media platforms, perhaps globally, perhaps in a certain district or city. These are all issues that the organisations which run brands have to consider every day in order to run their operations, but the due process that should exist for ensuring that the communications team is privy to all relevant information has historically been patchy, or the process for handling sensitive information has been inconsistent. Brands that aspire to having a finer sense of smell have to overcome that situation.

Being organised relies on some having eyes and ears, too, specifically systematic listening of digital signals and the foresight that can be gained by reacting to it early. We've already covered early warning systems, but the point is that the communications team does not have these senses in the same way that it did when reporting in the days of old media. Rather than reporting after the fact, brands have to develop systems and use tools for listening and observing that enable them to be at least as well informed on the conversations happening around them and about them as their audience. Cracks will always appear, but the more comprehensive the effort is the faster the brand can react, engage, counter and shift the conversation in its favour.

And then there's the mouth bit. The obvious part, but suffice to say that a brand that is engaging in conversation having listened and used its senses to see beyond the conversation that is now taking place will be in a far better position to say the right things and share the right information. It will already know what it's going to say before it opens its mouth, because it has used its senses in an appropriate way.

Providing, of course, that it's not kept mute by layers of approval hierarchy and indecision that were designed for offline media, but struggle or find it impossible to cope with deadlines that are simply as soon as the author presses 'send'. Equally, though, senior executives should not trust the communications team to simply communicate on behalf of the brand with just one thin layer of approval above them purely because media has changed and now they're far better at hearing what's going on around them. Like anyone in a business who's given responsibility for something important, there needs to be a plan.

We're not going to dive head-first into planning here. But the major ingredients of sound communications planning are substantial and all-crucial: a brand narrative, robust messages that are unique to the brand, an editorial content plan, integrated campaign plans and an arsenal of platforms and packages for both outbound and inbound communication. The planning needs to be far more sophisticated and intricate than communications teams have been able to operate within in the past – and senior management needs to understand the value of that planning just as it does comprehensive financial, operational or emergency planning. We're talking about the lifeblood of the brand, and clogged arteries aren't permissible.

With that degree of planning undertaken, what communications teams then need is trust from the top. They have to have the freedom, within agreed confines, to engage audiences and communicate. They have to be authorised to make judgement calls in tricky situations, providing they've done their homework and are acting in accordance with their job description. And just like personnel involved in other crisis situations, they have to be prepared to suffer the consequences of their actions if they get things monumentally wrong or fail to have lived up to the promises of their plans.

So communications has to be seen, and has to be authorised to operate, just like any other central business service that deals with really difficult stuff. It has to be well funded. It has to work to regulated, well-developed and clear processes. It has to operate in 'always-on' mode rather than jumping on things when they crop up. It has to be as resilient as it can possibly be, with the benefit of thorough understanding, robust operations, tried-and-tested practices and the ability to learn constantly from its actions.

And it has to be staffed by experts. But more on that in a few pages.

Fundamentally, the highly tuned and resilient communications team has to be structured with the absolute goal of being able to manage all risks and create all potential opportunities for the brand. It has to be able to achieve things for the brand that no other department can, rather than be a group of people who happen to have communications reflected somewhere in their job title.

In order to manage all risks, it needs to be conscious of everything that's going on in the world outside that could cause damage to the brand's reputation, perception or ability to operate. But it must also be aware of the whole truth and nothing but the truth of issues that occur on the inside, which means it must be trusted and in tune with the activity of senior management, in a way that no other business function probably is or can be. It cannot defend a brand properly unless it has full disclosure; warts and all.

In order to take advantage of all opportunities, a successful communications team needs to have the same all-seeing approach to the world outside, but it also needs to be empowered to act on opportunities when they fall into the brand's lap and when the brand can engineer them, either through conversation or through the inadvertent actions of others.

That takes trust, according to Louise Terry, international communications director of The Body Shop, in many ways one of the pioneers of audience engagement, and of building a brand story and reputation around its clearly stated values. 'In order to be a successful communications leader in-house, you need to build the trust of the most senior people so that they can rely on your judgement about the relative risks to brand or business reputation,' she said. 'Sometimes you have to act as the social conscience of an organisation, and be prepared to stand up and say that certain actions or behaviours are wrong because if they are not addressed they could affect reputation over the long term. You are like a kind of rudder keeping the ship sailing in the right direction!'

Public relations industry associations don't really offer any formal guidance or a best practice model for the structure and functional requirements of a modern brand communications team. Jane Wilson, CEO of the UK's Chartered Institute of Public Relations (CIPR), makes a distinction between the approaches of large multinationals and smaller firms, generally speaking. 'We could run social media and digital communications workshops every week and they'd keep selling out. But for many small to medium organisations, they often don't have this on their radar as they focus on brand building. The bigger companies tend to be far more savvy and do have this level of planning built into their resources and preparedness,' she said.

'I've seen some of the best examples of this pre-emptive approach in transport companies such as Transport for London.

The time is right to look at our digital, reputation and crisis training and see if there is a demand for some online protection training. The other interesting training area that this crosses over into is employee engagement. The starting point for many organisations is possibly that threats are external but as the HMV Twitter[32] example showed, sometimes the 'vandals' are inside the house.

'The intrinsic "value" of reputation and the ease with which it can be lost is definitely a growing concern and I see the more specific area of the online threat as a growing issue – in the profession and in business generally. But the delegates on our digital and social media training and events are perhaps less concerned with the "threat" that social media can bring to their brands as they are to opportunities of building brands online,' Jane said.

The PRCA is also working hard to bring some best practice to bear. Its CEO, Francis Ingham, points to its efforts to get to grips with the future of PR, the topic of its 2012 national conference in the UK. It has begun a long-term, fundamental assessment of what the industry needs in order to prosper. Over the second half of 2013, the association plans to ask PR people to vote on the recommendations contained in that piece of work. The result, Ingham hopes, will be clear guidance for how the modern team – both in-house and agency – should be structured and should function.

Effective mouthpiece of the brand

Becoming that effective communications service means leaner, meaner decision-making. The vast majority of communications people reading this will be thinking, 'interesting theory, but it

---

32 Sam Jones, 'HMV workers take over official Twitter feed to vent fury over sacking,' *The Guradian*, http://www.guardian.co.uk/business/2013/jan/31/hmv-workers-twitter-feed-sacking (January 2013)

takes me hours if not days to get stuff signed off'. What's our advice to them? Well, ultimately communications teams have got to grow a pair.

Because they need to force a change in decision-making, either through their positive actions or through frank conversations with management, or both. The way it really should work is that the communications team is trusted and empowered to communicate, and then gets on with it, in its entirety, for better or worse. In reality, that's rarely realistic when the sirens are wailing and the vultures are circling, but it really should be. The communications team should not have to ask the board what it wants to communicate; the communicators should already know. Equally, so the board should know that the communications team is on top of it and the threat or the opportunity is in the best possible hands. This may not always be feasible, but if decision-making models can work towards it, then we at least stand a chance. Other departments shouldn't be involved. Nor does everyone on the board need to have input – one person only should be given that responsibility. Lean, mean decision-making. Because there's no time for anything else.

Similarly, communications teams need to work towards this level of über-approval amongst themselves. Ideally, one person needs to be on duty at all times, on a rota basis, and poised to go out there and get the job done. It means taking a big weight on their shoulders; it's not a job for wimps.

Besides, who's actually doing the talking, anyway? The brand should be, surely? Right, but then again the brand exists in the minds of those who interact with it – it's not a real person. More often than not, a human being, rather than notional values attached to an inanimate concept, will be the one from whose mouth the words come.

Anyone with any connection whatsoever to the brand can,

officially or unofficially, be a spokesperson for it on any issue. But when it comes to fronting the brand in times of crisis, or steering it through to a positive outcome, it has to be either the person at the top of the business, or the person near the top, who's most relevant to do the talking. There's no avoiding it, and communications these days surely has to be a central part of any senior job. And that can be the undoing of many a best-laid communications crisis plan – the girl or guy at the top simply can't do the talking at the exact moment when the communications team needs them to do just that.

Which needs to change. Communications has to be equally as important as all other parallel corporate duties. And beyond the very sharp end of communications, when the brand is under attack and those at the top of the organisation are forced to respond, those corporate duties should also be resting on the shoulders of all personnel. The way that they share information publicly, reference the brand and strive to be consistent with the brand narrative all make a big difference. This unity can help to drive sustained, authoritative and authentic engagement with the brand's story, and so make it more difficult for vandals to take a lasting swipe.

The words that are chosen for the response should be traced to the communications team, but ultimately the communications team itself must trust everyone who represents the brand or is a third-party ambassador to disseminate them effectively. The messages and the brand narrative should be directed from the core of the business, but then all authorised people have to be let loose to engage audiences themselves.

This means a shift well beyond the conventional comfort zones of many communications teams. The reality in such crisis situations is that control is and has always been impossible. However, brands whose stories are led by strong communications teams that can interject directly in times of crisis or chaos have far greater command over reputation than any brand enjoyed before the advent of digital media, because so many forms of media are now two-way. That doesn't mean it always feels comfortable, though.

So the backbone of the story should be the responsibility of astute, progressive communicators who understand how to tell it, and more importantly how to entrust other people within the organisation others to help them tell it. The words used to tell the story should be inspired from the outset by the communications team but they then have to let go enough for others to be able to go and tell it their own way, with a little licence for alteration. Like all the best stories really.

A communications team that takes this approach and supports others in being the mouthpiece of the brand is doing all it can to apply process and knowledge to what brands need to be able to achieve in order to engage audiences – the art of conversation. The more fluid and free-rein the conversation can be, the more it will be credible, compelling and even absorbing. The more a brand can tell its story that way, the greater the moral and reputational defences it can amass against detractors. Without it, the brand is exposing itself unnecessarily and depending solely on on the nature of its business and its history may be something of a sitting target.

Constructive, fluid conversation should be the objective of those who are the mouthpiece of the brand. But they must have the systems, the authorisation, the cunning and the gumption to be able to take that conversation right to the door of detractors and counteract vandalism head-on. This won't apply to all conversations, but the more credit you've earned by engaging, sharing transparently and involving your most loyal supporters rather than holding them at arm's length, the better a position you'll be in.

The ingredients of five-star communications

What makes a brilliant communications team, then, one that is set apart from a merely competent communications team? Well the curious thing is that it's very hard to find good material on this, as so much in the past appears to have been entrusted to instinct and hope. Common sense counts for a lot, but it also needs direction and a support system.

The CIPR offers some pragmatic pointers. According to CEO Jane Wilson, brands now need communications teams that are forward-looking, quick to react in a positive way, opportunistic wherever possible and with a very strong understanding of the business objectives, structure and operations.

'It's a bit like manning a RADAR station. You have to first of all know what you're looking for so a good online tracking system that can identify conversations about your brand is a must, particularly if you are a multinational. You also need to make sure that the digital threat is part of your risk register and regular analysis, and that it forms an integral part of the crisis situation guidance. Finally, you must ensure that the leaders know where "the keys to the social media cupboard" are in order that they can take control in a crisis. Or to take an advantage of situation, as Oreo[33] did at the Superbowl,' Wilson said.

In short, communications is having to move from being largely an art to being a smarter and more potent fusion of art and science. And you need the right things in the right places.

The ingredients of superior communications capabilities are not subject to any statute. There are many professional standards bodies that offer recognised qualifications and set

---

33 Will Oremus, 'The Half-Decent Oreo Tweet That Dazzled a Nation.' *Slate*, http://www.slate.com/blogs/future_tense/2013/02/04/oreo_super_bowl_blackout_tweet_dazzles_twitter_reveals_low_bar_for_brands.html (February 2013)

standards for those who work in communications to adhere to. But for obvious reasons they're largely functional, or focused on sharing best practice. The raw ingredients of great brand communications go way beyond that.

The first ingredient, pretty clearly, has to be people who are great observers and curious about everything that is going on around them. They need to be brilliant – and patient –listeners, with the experience to be able to act appropriately on what they're hearing. Too often, listening skills and a predisposition to want to listen are highly underrated. They're not seen as nearly as glamorous as the big creative ideas that create fascination and can drive commercial advantage. But they should be – because without good listening, creativity can be misplaced or even counterproductive. Communicators also need to know which questions to ask, based on their experience and commercial astuteness. It all starts with knowing what people are saying, what they're likely to think and what rising threats may be lurking beyond the horizon.

In other words, active listening. Those are the character traits communications teams need in some of their personnel, but they also need to drive a desire for systems that monitor media and all conceivable threats to the brand. If you think about some of the attacks that have happened on brands in the past couple of years, none seem to have come completely out of left-field. All, with good monitoring, strong communicators and the engagement of the board in communications processes, could surely have been foreseen.

Next, five-star communications teams need people who are a strong combination of starters and finishers. Conventional team wisdom has it that people are either creative thinkers or completer-finishers, which may well be true but ideally communicators need to possess all of those skills, to varying degrees. And one of the most important areas where people need to start and finish things is audience understanding, the bedrock of commercially savvy communications and brand attack resilience. To understand audiences fully, brands need to go beyond having systems for tuning in and seeking feedback through engagement. They also need people who are technically literate, understand how to work with and interpret audience data in context and have a strong commercial streak so that they can spot the prospective advantages of what they glean from the audience and act on them.

The need to do this throws up an additional and somewhat contentious consideration. People who really get to grips with audiences and what motivates them are not necessarily all trained marketing or communications professionals. There is a strong case for the über-communications team to include people from very diverse backgrounds – not just those hand-picked to match core target audiences, but people with broad-ranging career experiences who can bring fresh perspective to understanding what's really going on out there.

Then comes the juicy bit; the content. The words and the pictures. The things that will drive sustained engagements through conversation, and that can actively encourage the audience to become more involved with the brand.

Powerful content is built by more than powerful creativity. Yes, communications teams need people with strong creative instincts and the ability to think abstractly. But they also need people who are inherently clever, with the persistent ability to conjure up new ideas. Historically, communications teams in some organisations have been something of a dumping ground for people who didn't cut it elsewhere in the organisation, or people who were very clever but became subsumed by the weight of internal bureaucracy, so spent most of their days negotiating politics and systematic barriers rather than applying their grey matter to challenges and opportunities. Not everyone in a communications team needs to be a brainbox, but great communications teams need to identify the really clever people and set them free to think about how to engineer really clever communications.

And there's no substitute for born cynics. The cynics need to provide the reality check on all of that. They need sound analytical brains, too, so that they can focus on audience understanding, but they also have to be tuned in to the natural cynicism of the audience to a brand wanting to talk to them, and the growing cynicism that can occur when people in social networks gang up together, when negativity becomes multiplied. A communications team without cynics is like a badly laden ship without an anchor.

Most obvious of all, communications people need to be good at communicating. You'd be surprised how many aren't. Every good communications team needs a few born orators, particularly those in the most senior positions. And they need to be able to sell; not in a product or service sales sense, but in their ability to tell a ripping yarn. Equally, strong orators don't all need to be types who present flawlessly in front of large audiences; that helps, but fundamentally orators have to be as enticing and entrancing when dealing with the audience one-to-one as they are one-to-many. And those many may be senior brand executives who need a better understanding of communications and why certain decisions have been made, so they'd better be able to think and talk on their feet, too.

Remember also that to be successful, communications teams need to be trusted by the brand to instigate and undertake communications on its behalf. Communicators need to be trusted to talk, and having characters in the team who are positive in the face of even the darkest adversity is a big help there.

Jonathan Copulsky at Deloitte adds one more ingredient: activation of the employee base. 'Research shows that employees are often more trusted than senior executives. Good communications requires that these employees understand the essence of the brand and are trained and willing to champion the brand in good times and bad. I'm astonished at how little effort most organisations invest in educating employees about the organisation's brand and what it takes to consistently deliver the brand'.

With all of those skills and personalities in place, communications teams will need strong leadership, just like any other team. With the change that has gone on in media in recent years, the emergence of more sophisticated techniques for attacking brands and the growing enthusiasm from the top for communications to have positive commercial outcomes, that leadership has never been at more of a premium. Leaders need to bring diverse, pressured and ever-learning teams together, get involved at the coal face wherever needed without micromanaging and appreciate that the communications function must innovate constantly in order to stay ahead and keep the brand protected.

Which means it's a job for the brave, but indeed valour is a trait that should run throughout the whole communications team. Chickens should go home. That courage needs to be ever-present when the team is working to build advantage through communications or at least maintain a market position, because the scope, scale and sophistication of sustained, engaged communications can send even the most hardened communicator dizzy at times. And at time of a brand attack, creative bravado and the guts to stick with it and see things through when reputational bullets are whizzing all around typically makes the difference between being weakened by brand vandals and emerging stronger.

Ingham says team skills are important, but so is common sense in orchestrating communication. 'Brand vandals don't sleep; and they are everywhere. Your most loyal customers can become the destroyers of your reputation – one might almost describe them as fourth-century Huns! So swift rebuttal, an understanding of social media, obviously, and also a deftness of touch are required. One personal example. Argos screwed up a toy delivery. I moaned online. Argos sorted it within 24 hours. In contrast, SW Trains implores you to follow the business on Twitter for on-board announcements, but doesn't say what the Twitter name is. Unsurprisingly, I praise one company and frequently vandalise the other,' Copulsky concluded.

In all, the ingredients of five-star communications are much the same as the ingredients of other winning teams: brains and balls.

Right direction at the intersection

Besides dodging or turning the tables of attacks on a brand, communicators also need to be able to rise above even brand issues to tackle an enormous opportunity – and risk – that has never been in shaper public relations focus: the intersection of brand and reputation. In the past these were managed as two separate things, or there were fewer potent opportunities to fuse them. Now the media landscape lends itself to some exciting but potentially daunting opportunities to jump into the fray and exploit the heady currents where brand and reputation cross streams.

The intersection of brand and reputation, and its fusion points with customer experience, is an exciting place. Because it can drive tangible purchase consideration and advocacy. But done wrong, it can leave brands and corporate reputations with egg on their faces.

Communicators – in fact most marketers – tend to talk about such a desired intersection as being amplification of purchase consideration or desiren. The reality can be more like an electric shock. Which is great, providing it shocks something into life, of course. While most communicators would probably concur that reputation has long driven purchase consideration in a more powerful way than the brand does, the added spark of brand can drive further advantage. Yet when faced with the threat of brand vandalism, the stark threat is that damage to the brand will trigger a slap in the face for reputation, too, and so drag both down together.

Which means that proactive efforts to meld brand with corporate reputation – and other direct points of audience influence – are set to become a highly desirable territory in public relations.

In short, it's all about making sure the brand has a persistent voice. And that means communicators don't just have to concern themselves with putting words in the brand's figurative mouth, but with shaping how the brand behaves ahead of, during and after opening its cake hole.

Says Copulsky's own work on this area: 'We've invested more in sensing, tracking, and research as online has become an important factor in shaping our interactions with clients and talent. We've also invested more in educating ourselves about appropriate communications and creating policies that balance among authenticity, responsiveness, and alignment with corporate objectives. Increasingly, we believe that what others say about our brand is as important as what we say about our brand and we want to listen to and influence the conversation.'

Getting this interaction of brand and reputation right, both by orchestrating it through planning and spotting opportunities to create it in response to events, requires a new type of collective mindset for communications teams. We've already pointed out that communicators coming from less conventional backgrounds may be a desirable thing; to get to grips with the intersection, the communications skills need to come from areas far broader than old-school media relations. People with skills in discipline integration – typically marketing, but also from other departments – people with frontline consumer engagement backgrounds, people with the ability to turn insight into intelligence and into ideas, and full-bore creatives, are increasingly becoming part of the desired make-up of communications teams, whether in a day-to-day sense or as broader project taskforces. So too are the data guys – the people who can use research and analytics to get inside the hearts and minds of the audience, and stay there.

Which means communications can be far more about certainty, and far less about hope.

Bad news for brand vandals. Providing the way the brand's stories are told, and how reputation is nurtured, is based on a solid foundation.

Authenticity: your story at the core

Many a wise public relations professional will tell you that reputation cannot be bought, it must be earned. True.

The same is true of authentic storytelling being the bricks and mortar of effective defences against brand vandalism. Authenticity cannot be bought, and cannot simply be achieved through the application of key performance indicators. It must be earned, and it cannot be earned unless every piece of content is genuine to the core.

At the core of authentic communications, through authentic storytelling, must be your story. Your brand's story, and one that wouldn't apply in the same way to any other brand.

The brand's story cannot be repurposed from someone else, or reshaped in the hope that it will become authentic. It won't be, and it may set you back, perhaps catastrophically.

This is all stuff that's difficult to argue with, as it's plain common sense. The challenge for many communications teams is knowing where to start the process, what value can be gained from previous communications and what the chapters of the story should look like, anyway.

According to the PRCA's Ingham, there's great interest in how to tackle online brand attacks, but too little knowledge. 'In one sense, it's a little like the situation with social media in general a few years ago – people know they need to be knowledgeable, but don't know where to turn for that knowledge. Obviously, interest and understanding differ from organisation to organisation, and in particular from sector to sector. The more sensitive your area of work, the more seriously you take brand vandalism,' he said. A clear brand story that sets out the brand's stall in full is a clear requirement, if only people knew where to start.

So what is your story? Well, children's books always tend to have beginning, a middle and an end. The brand's story is highly likely to have already begun, and only a communicator hell bent on career suicide would author the end.

Which leaves the middle bit, and that could meander uncontrollably, or expand like a gas to fill the void. Instead, what brands need to keep their stories on track is a strong and clear narrative to give an authentic story backbone. That narrative obviously needs to be unique to each brand, so that's something you're just going to have to figure out for yourself. And in order to build and tell a compelling, sustainable, engaging and even fascinating story with it, a few ingredients must be in the mix. One is clarity – which should go without saying, but equally it's all too easy to get clumsy and confused when telling a story when internal pressures and commercial forces come into play. Clarity, to another previous point, needs strong authoring skills and the ability to shield the story from unwise interference.

Relevance and the mechanical ability to engage are important too – the former driven by audience understanding and the latter by clever orchestration rooted in sound media understanding. With both set in stone, storytellers then need perhaps the single most important element of attracting and captivating the audience – the ability to paint a story in mental pictures rather than simply recounting it in a series of words. Anyone can document a story, but it takes a storyteller to be able to get the audience to envisage the story.

Regardless of what the appropriate story is for the brand and the ingredients that must be present for it to be well told, the one thing that must be slap bang at the heart of it is the truth. The truth of what, though? Put simply, the brand truth, or the brand difference as it's often called. The one single thing that the keepers of the brand have determined makes it truly different, and so the one thing above all that will cause, they hope, the target audience to like it, spend money on it and share positivity about it with others.

We'll stop going into the mechanics of how to deduce what the brand truth is, but suffice to say it must identify and filter the brand's vision, its history and its behaviour; its traits, its perception baggage and its intentions.

By going through that planning and analysis, brands will be able to determine or sharpen the focus on the one thing that is true about them, above all else. With that kernel defined, the brand story has the capacity to be told in an authentic way.

The path of authenticity will then be a long one, and probably never-ending. Take heart, though, because if you've got a communications team, a clear plan and the ability to tell your story well to an engaged audience, you've already got communications capabilities that are fit-for-purpose.

Pursuing authentic communications from that foundation takes an unwavering focus on the brand's core, connections and clout. They're the three legs of communications that can best protect the brand.

The core of the brand's story is anchored on distinctive truth that will be compelling to its audiences. Not because of well-informed guesswork, but because the brand's reputation guardians – the communications team – know it to be true. Because they've done all the right homework on the audience, the media and the content required to do the job.

Connected in that the brand's hard work to develop new connections and convert existing supporters to a degree of online engagement means that it has linked virtual arms with the very people who brand vandals are aiming to sway in undermining the brand: people who don't just trust the brand but believe wholly in it to the point of having unmovable faith.

Executing planned communications, driven by an expert team, means a brand can stand tall against its detractors rather than forever looking over its shoulder at where the attack might come from.

CHAPTER 11

RAISING THE ARMY

The perils of being along when the Internet attacks: advocates matter. #BrandVandals

About a decade ago, a new word began creeping into the common marketing dictionary. Advocacy.

Initially, it mostly meant brands seeking more comprehensive endorsement from customers who raved about their products or services. The ones who could be the best assets for editorial content, because when they vouched for the brand it was still plausible.

Social media has changed that. There has been a scramble for brands to want to be seen to be favoured by lots of customers, but in the case of merely chasing Facebook likes, it can soon look a little vacuous, or at least is becoming seen as very much first base.

What does advocacy mean, anyway? Well it's defined as the act of pleading for, supporting or recommending something, often through espousing it actively. That's actually a fairly broad range of actions – and pleading probably isn't going to do brand or reputation much good in the long run.

True advocacy, or at least any level of really meaningful advocacy in a brand and reputation management sense, runs much deeper. Because views are so easily shared and some people have gained a relatively strong level of influence over brand reputation, or discussions relevant to brands, in social networks, views have become more than fleeting observations. They have become opinion-forming statements that shape the perceptions of groups of people who the brand wants to build strong relationships with.

Which means advocacy has become a foundation layer of

reputation, and advocates are the building blocks.

Advocates are not necessarily the customers who spend the most money with the brand, or who shop most frequently. They may be someone who only bought the brand's product once, many years ago. They may not be able to afford it and so just aspire to own it. They may never buy from the brand, yet because of the respect they command and trust they have, they can make waves for you.

Advocates are a force to be reckoned with.

Your best customers are probably a good place to start looking for them. Most brands will have done this already and many have a long history of forging links with customer groups or individual consumers. With the Internet, and in particular with data from social media, they're easier to identify meaningfully than they ever were in the past. But customers alone will not make a solid advocacy network. For that, brands are realising that they need to connect to other groups and individuals, too. And then create a network that builds another layer of defence as well as a sound commercial platform.

Suppliers, partners, stakeholders, politicians, peer brands, competitors – yes, competitors – and of course the brand's own personnel are all desirable advocates for most brands. That doesn't mean 'the more the merrier', but it does mean that being able to hold up a group of loyal customers as a defence network when the brand is under attack will never be as effective as being able to count on the perspectives of people from all walks of life.

What brands really want them to do is be natural, be poised and then speak their minds. What brands don't want them to do – and nor should brands be tempted to do it – is to make it look like the band of advocates is on standby, on payroll and ready to jump to the rescue in the brand's hour of need. It doesn't need to appear to be natural; it needs to be absolutely natural.

Natural not just because they're left to their own devices, but natural because the relationship between the brand and its advocates is one that has been appropriately nurtured, with mutual understanding and respect, and never forced in any way. An unrealistic vision, because brands will always want to make a buck? Perhaps that might have been the view in the past, but today more enlightened brands tend to think differently.

That understanding and respect should be developed through listening, through learning and through rewarding advocates – in an appropriate way – for their support, and more importantly for their interest in the first place. Through listening, brands have to learn to make changes to their products and services as a result of what the advocates have to say. Ideally, they should become rock-solid advocates because they're not only engaged with the brands, but actively involved with them and helping to shape their future.

And brands should also want to recruit previous doubters or brand detractors and convert them into advocates. More difficult, probably, but where brands have really made the effort to address poor customer service or product problems, for instance, they have the opportunity to foster lasting, meaningful and vocal relationships.

According to Louise Terry from The Body Shop, however, having the trust of those advocates is also vital: 'Communications leaders need to have high levels of personal integrity in order to be accepted by external pressure groups, for example. They also need the intellectual skills and instincts to assimilate complex situations and present all sides of an argument to the different stakeholders. In my experience, the best teams I have worked with have demonstrated that ability to understand complexity, communicate simply, have the personal integrity and debating skills to be trusted and be personable enough to be liked'.

It's a people game.

Identifying the most important advocates

Finding the people who will become the more valuable advocates, and those who will do most to stand their ground for the brands when it's under the cosh, isn't easy. But it is possible, and in fact it's become more scientific.

It wasn't always that way. It used to be that the advocates were found either by chance, or through a laborious, manual process that was subject to never coming to fruition, anyway. It tended to rely on direct feedback mechanisms and then follow-up to confirm that the favour was genuine, or someone who knew someone who knew someone. Whichever route was used, and whether it was deliberate or not, the whole thing tended to either look manufactured, or be manufactured. Or both.

And how did the brands really know that they were the most important advocates that could be gathered? They didn't really. It was an art, rather than a science. At best, they were the supposed best advocates. Or, at risk of being negative, the best scraps that brands could scrape together. They were hardly an army of advocates, more an amateur sports team thrown together though circumstance with an ill-fitting kit and little in the way of common purpose.

It's not so much about whether they're genuine fans. It's more about whether they engage in the right way; not just say the right things, but do the right things and more importantly be connected to the right people in the right way. That engagement starts with conversation – with talking, rather than shouting. Rather than trying to trumpet things, they should be focused on communicating about, or around, topics.

According to Molly Flatt, a word-of-mouth evangelist for one of the longest-established digital agencies 1000heads, advocates can either have already shown their colours or can be best unearthed through some sensible lateral thinking. 'There are really two routes to identifying lasting advocates for a brand,' she said. 'For Nokia we're either looking for those people evangelising about a brand, a fairly obvious route. Where it gets really interesting is where we look for ways to identify people with whom the brand might have latent resonance and it's a case of making the connection.

'A simple example of this would be for the launch of Nokia's N8 we leveraged the product's superior video and imaging capabilities and built relationships with extreme sports communities who were passionate about getting out and shooting great video. Not obvious advocates at first but through the right approach and connection, they can become long-lasting brand advocates,' she said.

Simple, but effective. Because that's the sort of things that the vast majority of conversations are all about, particularly those that tend to create greater influence and that can have a lasting effect on reputation. People talk all the time, and the Internet has only increased their propensity to converse because – even more so than when the domestic telephone became mainstream, they can not only engage in chat with people who aren't present with them, they can talk to many people all around the world, whether they're known to them or not. They can also do so in new and, depending on your personal viewpoint, exciting ways.

Infiltrating those conversations is one part of what brands are seeking to do, and getting into discussions about topics that the target audiences cares about most, or are on new and emerging topics, is what brands have been attempting to do via regular media relations for decades. Only now, social media enables those conversations to be much more influential and owned media enables brands to say and do things that can be lined up for discussion in conversations.

The other thing that brands are seeking to do is identify the conversations and the participants in those conversations that, and who, will have their greatest net effect on their commercial aspirations. The same approach can apply to work to defend brands, as by identifying the most influential advocates, brands stand to build a stronger army.

'It really depends on how you qualify "most important",' says Flatt. Her team applies its experience of working in this area to a whole raft of criteria. 'We look at the volume, relevance, sentiment and engagement of both their content and their network, their stated behaviours, their offline influence and so on – in combination with intuition to select those who we feel are most suitable to work with on behalf of a brand.'

Brands also now have the opportunity to apply some proven science to an area that was previously the domain of art, a little guesswork and occasional luck. Their challenge is that there are simply so many conversations going on out there on the Internet, and indeed offline in response to topics covered across different media. In many cases, topics won't yet even have become relevant to brands, but could turn at any moment. Meanwhile, many tools are now available to search for and otherwise help identify the most relevant conversations and the people involved in them.

Using them to do the job well relies on more than just being able to have a topic flagged and then moving in on it. Context and nuance are crucial. Think of a conversation about road safety that a car brand might be interested in. It's a general one about the extent to which people feel safe because of the safety features in modern cars and the fact that none of the people in the conversation have ever had a serious accident. If they own that brand of car, some of those people may be good advocates. But perhaps other conversations about road trips with young children hold greater promise for advocate recruitment. The topic may not be specific to the brand's interest, but it's about driving generally. On further inspection, it turns out that because the road trip conversation is on a major and passionate parenting forum, and because 14 of the people who've contributed to the conversation have avoided serious injuries to themselves and their families in recent road accidents, and because nine of them drive the brand's cars, they are better engaged, better connected and more vocal communicators on road safety issues, and have first-hand experience of the quality of the brand's products. This is, of course, just an imaginary example.

That last part may have all read like the ramblings of an overzealous scientist, but you get the point. You don't only need to know where to dig; you need to know what you're looking at and why it's important when you come across something.

Context is crucial and assumptions should be tested. Planning can really pay off, and its value shouldn't be underestimated. And with the sophistication of social media analysis continuing to improve, and algorithmic tools now being used to give greater meaning to what can be found out about people online – not just who they are, but how they are influential and why they are influential – a more three-dimensional view of people can be readily assembled.

Building relationships with those people could easily take up several chapters in its own right. There is no magic formula, but again analytical tools can help to form a clearer picture of how prospective advocates feel about the brand and the topics around which they've been conversing. You can do a lot to deduce opinion, sentiment, passion and, through either explicit or implicit communications, the reason for it. All that can help brands to develop their plans for approaching or gathering the right people around them, starting to form a group of advocates and making sure that it has the right kinds of people in the right kinds of places to form a wall of defence around the brand, and be as ready as they can be to help deter or counter vandals when they strike.

Calling them to the rescue is a big decision, though, and you can't pull too many favours.

Should you pull the emergency cord?

Sometimes it's time to call in the cavalry. Knowing when you've gone past the point of no return is always going to be a tough judgement call to make, and one that few brands have had any practice at given the option has never really existed in the past. Will pulling the emergency cord be counterproductive in making you look guilty? Will there be enough fight in your army of advocates to see off the opposition? How can you be sure you're making the right decision given you're working under enormous pressure and being forced to make a decision very quickly?

It all depends which foot you're on. If you're on the back foot, you'd better hope you've done enough work with your advocates, and to build a resilient reputation in the age of new media, to be able to get back on an even keel pretty quickly. If you're on both feet, your position is better, but a rapid decision is still needed. If you're caught flat-footed by not being sufficiently prepared, you may well be out-manoeuvred. So the best place to be, as with most things in life, is firmly on the front foot.

In part that hinges on the decision-making process for this moment having been mapped out clearly in advance. The criteria for making the decision should have also been considered because you won't have time for much more than a quick-fire debate. Many brands have a highly developed process for making such calls in the event of a crisis, but equally, the decision to open up the situation to people beyond your walls can leave many an experienced communicator shifting nervously in their seat.

They shouldn't, because the reality is that well-managed advocates may be a better reputational asset in such situations than the vast majority of their own staff. Because they'll be credible, authentic and – if you've done your homework well – prepared.

Senior management will always want to be involved in the decision, but it should ultimately be taken by whoever makes the big calls on communications, unless the financial or political risk and reward involved is so large that for statutory or plain common sense reasons it should go to the person running the board. And remember that the vast majority of advocates, assuming they're glued to the brand's movements, will be completely conscious of the situation, anyway. They'll be expecting you to make a move.

It's also, perhaps, not a decision you'll even have to make, because advocates will have jumped to your defence of their own initiative and free will. Smart brands tend to realise that advocates who do just that are no bad thing, and such action is just another positive consequence of open, engaged business. In any case, letting advocates know that the brand could do with some help would rarely be something that would be communicated directly and explicitly – it would be too unsubtle, and because everything is on the record, the brand has to be prepared for those words to be shared with everyone. An implicit prompt is probably better, or at least a statement that demonstrates a combination of empathy with the audience and clarity around the reality of the situation. And in some cases, a firm denial.

There are ways of getting advocates to stand up and be counted that surpass any need for instruction. In the event of an unfounded brand attack, a strong move by the brand to counter the allegation and take a sharp jab at detractors is highly likely to cause advocates to leap to their defences. While it may mean rolling with the punches, the stark reality is that the more emotive the issue in hand, the more attractive an entry point it will be for brand vandals to do their work but the more fired up fans and vocals are likely to be. If you've built a strong community of advocates, their action and their influence should be practically second nature.

It's also worth thinking about how you can test the reflexes of your advocates before the moment comes. Not so much through a communications fire drill, but through their activity that is part and parcel of your communications plan anyway. The brand should be involved in real-life conversations and in order to fuel the engagement of the audiences, those should sometimes tackle contentious issues. After all, the audience will be talking about them anyway. Being involved in those conversations, and being at the forefront of steering opinion around them, gives brands the best possible workout for dealing with deliberate acts of sabotage and gives their audiences an opportunity to show themselves as either allies to the brand, indifferent or somewhere in between. It means they're likely to show their true colours, more so than through most kinds of primary research.

And because you'll have shown your true colours, and your opinions on contentious or related matters, they'll know where you stand, too.

Equally, if the opinion of advocates is divided in these fact-gathering missions, that's probably a good thing because at least you'll know where you stand. It may feel like a risky endeavour, but you'll know far more about your audience and far more about their likely capacity to come to your aid than you ever would have done before the Internet. And you never know, it might even make vandals think twice about trying it on in the first place.

Rather than letting a debate to rage out of control, it's far better for it to take place where you can see it, and with the knowledge that some of your staunchest allies will either get drawn into it or can be roped in by you if you need to. The debate will happen anyway, so better for it to happen in an environment where you've thought about the participants, primed them with information and know the ropes.

What if vandals masquerade as advocates?

But two can play that game. It's completely conceivable that vandals could infiltrate advocates and even masquerade as them in order to learn the brand's communications plans, particularly for anticipated questions, and turn the tables. And realistically, how would brands ever know the difference?

They won't. Not unless detractors show their hand in advance, and the smart ones won't do that. It would be a little like undercover police operations, with some operatives being so deep undercover that they can become impossible to spot. Worse still, some of the people who aren't vandals but can get caught up in the furore when an attack happens may actually be people who typically like the brand. There are few examples of this happening to date, and you've got to ask yourself why people would even bother, but it's feasible that someone somewhere might opt for mischief.

If they do, the best way to try to root them out is to apply the same techniques that are used on the flipside to identify the strongest advocates: a mixture of science and its persistent appliance, so that they're targeted in context. Some will always slip through the net, but the more diligent the planning and analysis to enable the brand to truly understand who it's dealing with, the more the threat of vandals can be cut down to size. The more information is applied to root out bad people, the more a similar level of information can be applied to identifying the positive, engaged people who counterbalance them.

It cuts both ways, and ultimately it's all down to the power of the crowd; to sheer weight of numbers. If that weight happens to include people who are really influential and really well connected to the conversations that will make the most difference, more's the better. The more open and willing the brand is to involving itself in the discussion, and the more it has got itself ready for that, the better a position it is likely to find itself in. To an extent, it's about beating them at their own game and not being phased. Whereas brands previously could retreat to the comfort of their ivory towers, that's no longer possible, but equally the brands that do most to engage are the ones that are most difficult to dislodge. Vandals are likely to expect brands to retreat into their shells when they land the first punch: come out transparently, and with a large swathe of advocates influencing the debate, you can hold the majority of the cards. You're being goaded by transparency, and if you can be even more transparent, you can at least take a firm footing in the discussion.

Ultimately, the crowd will either decide or will have the greatest day in the decision. The more people you have on your side, and the greater influence they can have over others who matter to you, the better.

There can be ways to single out detractors who've posed as advocates, too. Fundamentally, it'll be pretty obvious what they're up to. If they're seen to be deviously burying themselves amidst fans, playing along with the assumption that they support you and then turning against you, it's a pretty dirty way to go about things. And that's what most of the rational people you want to communicate with are likely to think. Transparency not only forces a greater degree of honesty, it can also encourage an expectation of fairness. Vandals that use dirty tricks to try to poke holes in the defences of brands may well be held to account by the very audience they're trying to sway.

Transparency places an onus on brands and their detractors to be equally above board. It's a game everyone must play, because it's so easy for anyone trying to be mischievous to be found out. It means that the playing field is as level as it can be. And it means that while vandals may lurk in the reeds, the more transparent and engaged the brand, the more likely it is that they will have to show themselves. If they don't, and they're caught in the act, it could be a short-lived protest.

If the situation does drag on, the issue has the potential to become inflamed, but there are still ways and means of dealing with it.

The main thing that brands who are being attacked have going for them in such situations is that they may be at the epicentre of a potentially enormous, sensitive and exceptionally difficult conversation, but the same rules apply as do to all conversations. Eventually, if the same thing is just repeated over and over again, with no new information and no one else really joining the conversation, most people will get bored of it. The brand's advocates and detractors may revel in some seemingly salacious information for a while, but providing the brand has attained some degree of command over the story and the advocates are being both vocal and influential, all the right things should be in place to diffuse the talk.

The risk here is both about the damage done to reputation – and potentially sales – initially and the lasting tarnish that may result. There is nothing the brand can do about the fact that the attack has happened, but the more it can use advocacy to its advantage, the more it can bring its point of view forward in the conversation, and the more the brand's perspective is likely to be a lasting part of the story's legacy. Or if it really managed to knock the vandals off their perch, it could make it a story that was quickly forgotten. Better still, it could make the brand come out on top if it's seen as having tackled the problem responsibly, fairly and by taking the moral high ground.

It could be the vandals who're left humbled.

Keeping the army fed and watered

It takes a sustained, concentrated effort to maintain this level of advocates in the background or the foreground of conversations around the brand. And like any conversations, interest levels and chatter cannot be maintained at a constant level indefinitely. Even the biggest gobs around need a break every once in a while.

Advocates can't be kept in barracks. They can't be kept on high alert. For the vast majority of time, like emergency volunteers, really, they're just going about their normal business. Which is a good thing, because normal people with no axe to grind make the best advocates. Because they're true advocates.

The brand needs to keep them permanently engaged, though – just at the right level. They need to be 'snacking' on the brand's story and involved with it through a tailored kind of engagement, not a bias but a special kind of relationship that acknowledges their respect for or support of the brand, and the level of influence they have in the social circles they move in. That can take many forms, of course, but brands need a sustainable strategy to achieve it. It's basically a big insurance policy for the brand's reputation, but if it's well orchestrated then that deep, persistent engagement with such an important part of the audience can drive commercial benefits well beyond the maintenance of positive reputation.

Management of the conversation takes both resource and an understanding that the advocates can't be controlled, nor can the brand become invasive in their lives. There is a line that can't be crossed, and only brands that really understand their audience and take a pragmatic approach to engagement can be expected to always stay on the right side of it. The whole thing needs to be anchored on trust, respect and above all a level of familiarity that brands only used to be able to dream of.

According to Flatt, some basic ground rules can go a long way, and working out how best to sustain the relationship relies, more often than not, on common sense. 'We need to remember that we are dealing with people here. Measure yourself based on how you act in relationships in your day-to-day life. This really is about one-to-one relationships – we speak to advocates on a regular basis and maintain an ongoing dialogue with them. It's no good simply sending them a new project or involving them in a new campaign and then once it's finished, walking away.'

Advocates like this can be such an important asset that conventional marketers can be forgiven for feeling they want to keep the asset under wraps, given it could be a strong competitive advantage. They can't. It will be practically the same process for competitors, for example, to identify who a brand's best advocates are as it is for the brand itself. In fact, those people may be fans of a whole bunch of brands, many of them competitors. In the case of an attack, it really doesn't matter.

And in fact it can be to the brand's advantage for it to be known as generally well-liked, given that this makes it a more difficult proposition to attack in the first place. It doesn't make it impossible but it becomes a bigger wall to climb. This is all providing that the brand doesn't have any serious skeletons in its closet, or become involved in business that poses a threat to its reputation.

A more common threat, and one that is very difficult to plan for, is the development of a story utterly beyond its control. If the brand becomes wrapped up in something purely because it operates in the same sector, because it's not crystal clear in its communications when the story takes flight or because it's just plain unlucky, then it can find itself on the back foot with a storm in its face very quickly. In that case, it will need advocates more than ever, fired up and ready to help in the counterattack, and if they feel the attack is unjustified or unfair, they won't need to be asked twice.

Healthy, open discussion lies at the heart of sustained advocates. Healthy because it's about the things that the audience really wants to know about or have a conversation about, and open because it's both transparent and the subject of genuine two-way interaction between the brand and its audience.

The communications team, or its extended team, has to look after that and be responsible for it, but there are others within the business who should probably be involved in the effort. Ideally, every interaction that the brand has with its most important influencers should be prioritised, as a disconnect between communications and, say, service or support could be counterproductive.

No brand can be perfect, but the more integrated its efforts can be to manage and sustain a community of ardent supporters, the better its reputational defences will function.

Asking soldiers inside

When things get frothy, advocates should therefore be ready to respond. Some progressive, brave brands can go even further than having the army primed by having their soldiers be directly involved with the brand's activities.

It's a big step, but one that can make defences stronger and create a bank of influencers, who not only back the brand but spend with it. Influence and protection can be fused with a traceable sales cycle. Such techniques are in their relative infancy in the age of fragmented, digitised media, but the principles are becoming clearer. By hand-picking a group of advocates based on their expressed likes and views, behaviour and level of influence, brands can create a community within an audience that can not only be useful for external communications but can actively help shape the success of the business and its activities. It goes beyond open business and into the realm of inclusive business.

In fact it goes a bit beyond inclusion. Do it right, and brands can turn inclusion into inspiration.

It's blindingly obvious that few people really like to be sold to, and that the evolution of media has made this dislike even more acute. But it's also obvious that people who like a brand or even obsess over it stand to be dazzled by it if they're given special access to it. Even more so if they're actually listened to, and their input helps to shape what the brand does. Rather than interrupting the lives of their best customers and most valued supporters, brands need to interact in them.

Marketing history is littered with examples of brands succeeding by listening to their customers and even allowing them to steer product and service development directly. Remember Tom Hanks, the toy inventor in the film *Big*? Okay, a pretty poor cultural reference, but hopefully you get the point. Let the most vocal supporters bathe in the brand and they won't just love it a bit more, they can become fanatical.

Active involvement is highly likely to equal active advocates. It sows the seeds of stories, stories that are compelling and are influential, not just because they're newsworthy but because the people at the centre of them are themselves influential. It's a step into uncharted waters for many brands, but the alternatives of distance from the audience and disengagement from their prospective vocal and influential support surely has to be a risk that brings the fear of the unknown into razor-sharp focus. Advocates can not only be on standby, they can be always live, ever-ready and doing their utmost to quash any dissent as it arises.

Not a bad return for simply letting some hardcore fans into your world every once in a while, in a fairly controlled environment.

It makes it even more crucial, though, that brands don't keep secrets from them, or seek to distort the facts in order to earn what is probably undeserved favour. There can be no secrets. Trust and respect must be upheld at all costs and there must be no attempts whatsoever to interfere with how advocates seek to communicate their engagement to the outside world. Instead, brands have to be comfortable with them expressing their thoughts and feelings authentically. As in honestly.

Flatt shares the view. In her experience, advocates who morph into brand advisers can only serve a purpose when their involvement is genuine. 'It's about being honest and realistic. Clearly on paper allowing brand advocates to input into R & D looks great. However, it often isn't doable because of operational and commercial realities. If you are going to allow people to influence your business, you need to show them that their opinions are being heard and they are having some sort of impact. Otherwise it's just hot air,' she said.

Giving the best advocates privileged information should actually become part and parcel of their kinds of active engagement. It's an event worth considering – trusting the most trusted advocates with information that should really be kept private, providing that if it does leak into the public domain then its effects will be minor. Sound crazy? Well consider the level of positivity and advocacy that something like that might drive. It's all just common sense, really, as this kind of behaviour and these kinds of techniques are what human beings do all the time in physical conversations.

Special treatment can go a long, long way. It can create otherwise unprompted conversations amongst target audiences, regardless of what the advocates say or do about it. Equally importantly, it drives reputational gain because the perception of the audience is improved. And the reason for that is because of how the brand is behaving and how it's seen to behave, which, after all, will have the greatest single impact on brand reputation. The transparency of digitised media has only heightened this effect.

What brands really need from their advocates at their hours of need is simple: the road of the crowd enticed by the talk and the actions of those most in the know. You want them to stand shoulder to shoulder to support you, but that can only happen if there has been careful planning and sustained commitment to keeping advocates supportive through a deliberate policy of engagement.

How far the brand chooses to engage is down to personal choice and circumstance, but it's by now surely crystal clear that without engagement, there can be no advocates. There is a lot that most brands can learn from how sorting teams manage their fan bases, and how hardcore fans have long been seen as special, worthy of different treatment and a deeper level of effect.

Engagement needs to be real, not fleeting, vacuous or tied to a purely quantitative metric. It needs to be genuine, and that itself needs to be tested. It needs to be opportunistic, and carried out free of the fear of interjecting into conversations with advocates, or with other participants in different but relevant conversations. There is a lot to do, and it does take time to nurture the most powerful advocates, but the stakes are high and the benefits undisguisable.

Let's face it: without advocates, you're pretty much on your own. That's not only uncomfortable, but potentially perilous.

CHAPTER 12

BATTLE-READY IN 90 DAYS

Know thine enemy. Or be at the mercy of the sewer.
#BrandVandals

There's clearly no better time to start than the present. And for many brands, maintaining effective defences is a permanent job, not a one-off project. But there are steps that can be taken to get a reasonable level of protection in place in just a few months. They won't be fit-for-purpose, but they could well show you where else defences need to be built, and at least give you some basic cover.

You can get battle-ready in 90 days, we think. You may not win the battle, but better to set yourself up for a war by being able to get a good look at the enemy and assess your own weaknesses while you're at it.

The first thing to recognise is that constructing defences against online brand vandals should not be a parallel activity to what you've built up as systems and best practice for handling crises that break in regular media. This is not an additional activity; it's one massive upgrade in sophistication, agility and mindset from how crisis management was undertaken in the past. On the bright side, though, the clear and present danger that saboteurs represent in the Internet age and the blindingly obvious commercial risk of not being able to at least fight back when they strike means that the insurance policy of investing in protection should at least, in theory, be easier to sell to those to the top.

There is no such thing as a digital crisis versus a regular crisis. Today, all crises are digital because all media is potentially digital, just as all information is potentially digital. In fact, we should stop thinking of stuff as digital at all. This is the modern world, and this is modern media. Deal with it.

You'll need a team, of course. Not just a team from the communications department, but people who are brought into the process or at least kept informed of it from senior management, operations, finance and customer services. Firstly, you'll need support from the very top, or at least from the person near the very top who will foot the bill and deal with the financial fallout if things do go pear-shaped.

That team should really be a core team – the people who will form the nucleus of a response team once you've become battle ready, and the people who are in the obvious roles that should get engaged in both forming defences and acting on attacks. They also really must be people whose existing job descriptions mean they have a lot to lose, as well as something potentially to gain, from the actions of detractors.

The first thing you'll need to do is get them on board. Make your 90-day exercise clear to them in detail and let them know when you'll need their services. That's easier said than done, but perhaps a wise way to go about it is to have a clear, commercially logical goal that you want to achieve by the end of the period. That might be to be able to navigate a simulated attack, or to be able to apply some kind of commercial acid test to the outcome of the exercise so that some notional value can be attached to the capability that has been created. Circumstances will vary, but there needs to be a firm purpose in your sights. And you need to have a strong stomach.

So what do you want to achieve? Again, that will vary, depending on where you're starting from, and what the brand is or does. The most likely objectives will be a thorough assessment of risk and capability, plus putting some basic systems and defences in place so that the brand emerges better protected. Or it could be that you're well on the back foot, so just having the ability to engage the audience directly and respond faster than you're currently able to should be the focus.

You may have a more political rationale. It could be that you want to use the exercise as a test case for securing funding and support for a sustained counter-crisis capability. It could be that you want to put the communications team through its paces and, at the risk of sounding a little cruel, sort the wheat from the chaff. Or maybe this is a form of pressure-testing, so the communicators can work out where in the organisation the weak links exists.

All might have a place on the list of objectives for any pragmatic brand.

In pursuing them, it's important not to take your eye off the ball and remember that while you're busy practising how to cope, the threat to the brand remains very real. And if anyone amongst the enemy gets wind that you're going through the exercise, you'll be a fairly soft target.

The best advice here is to plan a 90-day assessment and short-term overhaul that both achieves the most pressing objectives and enables the communications team to assess comprehensively what else remains to be done to make all reasonable improvements to make the brand more resilient in the face of attacks. And even if this short period of time will enable giant strides to be made in providing cohesive protection, the exercise will still need to do much to determine what ongoing activity is required to help ensure the brand stays reasonably protected, rather than risks increasing over time.

For these reasons, a project like this to toughen existing defences, apply social media systems to an existing crisis and issues response approach or formalise what has previously been a flimsy and informal set of practices is best carried out by a special team. It can be a small group of people from within the communications team, perhaps an external agency or a combination of both. It could, and perhaps should, involve people from other parts of the organisation, too. That way it stands the best chance of being a focused effort that doesn't get distracted, but also means the main communications team, having been briefed on the project, can get on with its day job while the walls are examined and tested.

Seeing over the hill

'This team must be capable of seeing around corners.' 'We're looking for an approach that gives us unprecedented foresight.' 'We need to always be able to see what's coming over the next hill.' Look like familiar phrases?

That's because communications briefs and requests for proposals tend to be littered with them these days. That's because everybody wants to gain capabilities that allow them to plan ahead in the event of a crisis or of a looming opportunity, and everyone wants to try to counter the pressure to increase operational agility with a little slack being cut.

The reality is that the ability to see clearly and far into the distance is tough, if not impossible, in brand communications. Some things can be predicted, other things can be foreseen with some reasonable guesswork, but most things either fall into your lap, crawl up your trouser leg or slap you around the face.

Seeing around corners and over hills is only possible with the application of tools. Monitoring systems, smart data analysis and a rigorous process can help in making a brand poised for dealing with an onslaught of vandalism, but there is no magic machine that can give extra foresight. The most important thing is to be able to smell the enemy coming, or hear their footsteps. And to do that, you need to recognise that you have enemies, find out who they might be and learn to deduce the telling signs that they're on the prowl.

As we've already covered, brands in contentious sectors, sectors with a history of dissent or brands that themselves have had prior experience of being metaphorically shot at by detractors are ones who should find identifying their enemies fairly straightforward. But all brands have far more stones that need to be turned over in order to assess who might want to take them down a peg or two. The backgrounds of their senior executives, partners, alliances and partnerships, investments, subsidiary operations, planned strategic initiatives, supply chains and operational safety all play a part in reputational risk and any one could form an avenue of attack. Sometimes the smallest hole in the wall is the best way for vandals to break in, so even a seemingly minor issue should be considered on its merits. It's a lot of ground to cover, and amounts to the brand having to be utterly honest with itself, with nothing concealed. No stone should be left unturned, because stones that annoy the audience are likely to be thrown back hard by the enemy. Which may just sting, but can render you unconscious.

Monitoring tools are fundamental here. Not just the oft-asked question of which social media monitoring tools will be most effective, but the application of a transmedia approach that embraces all media channels for content and comments relevant to the brand, and indeed those that aren't currently relevant but either represent a substantial reputational risk or would be a smart place to start an attack from in order to see it snowball. Most of the content assessed will be online, but don't discount the offline content. Instead, everything should be drawn into one place so that a single, radar-like view of what's out there can be gained.

Communicators also need to learn to interpret that data so that it's seen in context and the risk can be accurately assessed, based not just on what is being said, but who has said it and how they're connected to others. In just 90 days, it's impossible to expect that such an intricate system can be established and become operational, but with sound planning and application a team should be able to get to first base. It should be able to take a comprehensive and cohesive view of the media landscape, evaluate the required tools for the most immediate priorities and introduce them to communicators with at least some basic instruction in how to use them, and with a few managers given a crash course in greater expertise so they can ultimately teach the others.

All of this should be extremely useful in showing where the weak spots are, some of which the brand may have never even considered. It may find out things that no one even knew about its people and its partners. It may unearth connections and conversations on the Internet that had seemed innocent enough, but combined to a growing web of dissent. It may show that a newspaper or radio outlet is becoming increasingly feisty on an issue that will become more pertinent for you, so should be factored into communications planning in the future. It may show you nothing that you didn't know already, but you'll have gained a media command centre that finally draws everything into once place and helps to diminish that nervous apprehension that any moment something could be published that gnaws a big chunk of your reputation's backside.

Above all, working out where you're most vulnerable combined with the ability to gain greater listening powers, through media monitoring, and better smelling powers, through contextual analysis, will allow you to better predict forthcoming threats. It won't allow you see right over hills or around corners, but it'll give you enough of a view, and will bring some science to your apprehension of what might be lying out there unseen, or what kind of storm might be starting to brew.

But preparation isn't everything. Working to get a much firmer grasp on what's out there is only really useful when communicators are granted the power to act. And for that, they need the support of others.

Gaining internal buy-in

The first obstacle to gaining the buy-in of senior management, departments and other colleagues who are involved in enabling communications to happen is getting everyone involved to be clear on what risks are faced. This needs a prescriptive approach. Simply stating that risks exist or that media change has brought with it a new world of threats isn't going to cut it. And while the examples of other brands that have suffered at the hands of vandals can help to form a convincing case, there's no substitute for a set of clear statements on risk that cut to the chase and pinpoint exactly how what's out there poses clear and present danger for the core activities of the business. Not just, 'Unless we keep the vehicle well maintained there's a risk it could become unroadworthy and strike a tree in the case of a poor driving decision,' but, 'The brakes will last another 25 miles and after that we won't be able to take a corner at anything more than 20mph without killing the car and causing ourselves death or serious injury.'

Tackling the most pressing risks with investment of money and time is an exercise best anchored on raw and accurate facts.

In order to be in a position to understand the true nature of those risks, communicators need to ensure they understand what is most crucial to the business. To what extent are things like shareholder faith, daily sales, brand trust, partnerships and staff morale important? They're all important, but what is the order of priority and what level of value is attached to each? Again, these are the kinds of questions that should be asked as part of any sensible crisis management development exercise, but they're not always scrutinised to the level they should be. While organisations in exceptionally high-risk industries, such as nuclear energy, chemical production and drugs testing will look long and hard at such considerations, the quantifiable impact of less visible or perhaps less obvious risks in other sectors can be subjected to too little consideration.

Better to think 'What's the worst that could happen?' and then multiply it several times until it forms the basis of your worst conceivable nightmare.

Confronting others with such stark scenarios means you'd better be prepared with a clear plan as to how such risks can be managed. Given the 90-day scenario this will probably look like a project plan that sets out how you'll go about completing the project, your purpose and what will be delivered. Included in that list of deliverables should be a further plan setting out what else will need to be done in order to round up its defences and ensure that risks don't end up increasing because over time those defences become less effective.

This puts a big onus on being able to turn around that initial plan and having the time to talk it through with those internal stakeholders quickly. If you're really going to turn this level of capability improvement around in 90 days, dithering and delaying aren't an option. These risks are so fundamental that unless you've already got something that needs tuning rather than a round of improvement, people should just have to make time, and you need to get your skates on with that plan. It will need to cover all the things that good plans do: why you're doing it, who's involved, how you'll do it, when you'll do it, how it will need to be supported and how much it will cost. Most important of all will be your objectives and how success in achieving them will be measured. It will all need to add up to a definitive improvement in reputational defences, rather than just something that is probably better than what went before it.

If all of this is done to the letter, and you're successful in getting the level of support you need, then justifying the investment should be a walk in the park, shouldn't it? In theory, yes. In reality, unless the risks have already made themselves apparent and the brand is either already on the back foot or has had to defend itself in the past, appreciating the risk and what needs to be done to tackle it can be a challenge unless the right people are listening. Think of those scenes in *Jaws* where the mayor refused to close the beaches because he wasn't convinced just a few initial shark attacks meant that a hungry, oversized monster was sploshing about just beyond the shallows.

In your favour, the risks to reputational damage and hence commercial or political fortunes will always far outweigh the investment needed to provide adequate protection against them. It's an insurance game, but the rise of digital media actually helps to paint a clearer picture for those who need a currency symbol in front of every risk statement, because the ability to see how attacks are likely to unfurl and who in the audience would get roped in can draw some actual, or if not some very firm theoretical, correlations between reputational threat and financial exposure. By the end of the 90 days, if the brand were in severe need of better protection it is likely that investment will need zero justification. They might even be falling over themselves to thank you for all you've done to bring the risk into sharp focus and tackle it head-on. Perhaps.

Fast-track engagement

There is no substitute for genuine, meaningful, two-way engagement between brand and audience. But realistically, that's going to take time to develop into layer upon layer of staunch advocates and other people engaged with the brand who can scrutinize or stand up for the brand when it's under attack. In fact, it'll be a never-ending assignment as audiences evolve and change.

In order to go from a fledgling, patchy or even non-existent level of audience engagement to something that, in less than three months, can be an asset that adds a layer of protection, the communications team is going to have to pull a few tricks. Not buying sympathisers, not just issuing a rallying cry to family and friends to be ready to help out. Well, perhaps the latter may have a little place in your plans, but you can hardly rely on it to save your bacon.

The question of who to engage isn't one that can receive a consistent answer across every brand. There is no one-size-fits-all here. But here are some of the groups a smart brand can look to draw support from by roping in people from existing conversations and approaching others with a reason to get involved in some form of dialogue or information-sharing. Firstly, colleagues: an obvious one, but crucial. Next, trustworthy partners, analysts, advisors and suppliers. A small cross-section of your target external audiences, based on a concerted effort to identify the most positive people using analysis of social media conversations, which should also arm you with the intelligence to know which are best steering clear of because they're cantankerous or obstinate. Finally, if your media relations machine is up to it and the nature of your business activity makes it appropriate, some journalists who are influential and who you know will appreciate being kept informed on the brand's activities beyond merely chasing editorial.

That'll all least give you a crew to work with. Not much of one, but it'll be a start.

You'll then need to work with those people to engage them in your brand's activities and, ideally, its central story so that they're interested, hopefully supportive and if so should be as well placed as they can be in the timeframe to act as ambassadors on your behalf. Ambitious, yes. But feasible, providing you have your sights clearly set on your objectives and take a frank, pragmatic approach to engaging people. Rather than bringing advocates on board progressively over that period, it also makes sense to assess what you're dealing with soon after the first orchestrated 'recruitment' push.

A four-week focus, or at least some market that is set down less than halfway through the project, is good advice here. A week in and you won't be able to see the bigger picture yet, but after a month has passed you and your team should be able to quantify and qualify those who you've sought to engage, and begin to see some early signs of how they're reacting in the course of conversation about topics that matter most to the brand.

To do that, you're going to have to give them a reason to talk; to stir things up a little.

It's highly unlikely that you'll be able to do this by referencing the fact that you're trying to build a bank of supporters quickly so get the brand's defences off the back foot. In fact, doing so would almost certainly be tantamount to reputational suicide. Yet there are certain things that the brand can look to say and do that should smoke out loyalty and disloyalty, and favour and indifference, from the audience you're trying to bring closer. It may be that making a position clear on an issue that you've been deliberately hazy on up until that point can help to stir support and respect. It may be that a little self-criticism can go a long way. There's no substitute for humour, one of the most powerful communications tool there is. Anything is worth considering, and you won't have much time so the tactics must be chosen wisely, but clever communicators will be able to split things that are both evocative and a bit provocative in order to not so much turn heads as open some ears.

And some mouths. Well, actually, it'll be more a case of getting some fingers tapping on keyboards and punching those annoyingly small interfaces on smartphones and tablets. The more you can get people to speak up, the more you'll be able to gauge which people will be most important to the brand at a time of crisis, and the more you'll be able to gauge how they'll be likely to react if a problem occurs. It should also become self-perpetuating, because there's no better way to understand what the brand should do or say to elicit certain reactions from the audience than to gain a detailed understanding of that audience. The more you know, the more you'll know what to say, and the more you'll learn. Just like with any conversation.

You'd just better have big ears to listen with and eyes in the back of your head to see problems coming, which means that evaluation systems and engagement tools had better be fit for purpose. Having completed a detailed check on progress after a month, the brand should be making strides towards achieving its aims within three months. Over the remaining two months, it should look to do ever more to connect its central story with the audience it is seeking to harness. Rather than any attempt to tell the overall brand story, which would be impractical and probably raise questions about your intentions, picking on one or two story points within the overall story and working those hard amongst your audience is probably wiser. Package it as a juicy bone to gnaw on, then throw something else into the mix to get the pulse racing as well. However you do it, the main consideration should be that you pick stories and issues that will best help you to unearth the people you'll want to keep closest to you, which invariably will mean picking things that cut right to the heart of the brand's purpose, activity, history or vision. In other words, it'll have to be emotional stuff, within reason.

Testing the defences

Testing all of this within the three months make logical sense and is surely the only way to really assess whether defences have improved. The question is whether testing is actually feasible, as rocking the boat would run the risk of alerting the brand's opponents, surely? Well that's a risk anyway, and providing you've mitigated that risk to the minimum possible and are on high alert in case an attack happens, testing is completely practical.

What are you testing for, then? Ultimately, you're looking to assess the level of resilience that the brand has to hitherto unseen attacks from detractors, so that it can respond without lasting damage where an attack is unwarranted, or with minimal damage where an attack is warranted and some form of corrective action will need to be taken by the brand. Sounds simple, doesn't it? Well it isn't, but there are a few things that should be the focus in order to make the testing meaningful and useful.

Firstly, test how people react and how they interact with each other in coming to your aid. Equally, identify those that give no support, and those that start to turn against you, which is never comfortable but at least you'll know where you stand. Then look at how your own people react as you'll be able to address them directly, to an extent, afterwards. Evaluate how fast your communications team responds and what decisions it chooses to make. And most importantly, watch what your rivals and opponents do.

What kind of test should you undertake? Well you're not going to want to aim a missile at the ship just to see whether it misses, but it has to be pretty purposeful. It can't be like a conventional mock crisis conducted to test media relations capabilities in a safe haven environment either – because the defences you've built are very public and so will be any exercise you carry out. Instead, the best you can do will be to let loose something that's ultimately harmless but that is likely to prompt a reaction from your audience that can be assessed meaningfully. It won't be anything like a real attack, but it will at least give you an indicator of communications performance and tell you who your friends are. Bear in mind, though, that a real crisis may erupt in the middle of your efforts to test your ability to respond to such a scenario, so you will always need to be on your guard. But the whole point of this 90-day exercise is to improve your defences quickly, and the alternative is to sit on your hands waiting to be shot at, which is pretty undesirable.

What you should be concentrating on here is listening, responding and analysing, which are the three core tenets of engaging in conversation. Once you have an audience to talk to, you want to talk to them. You want to be smart in how you respond to comments and what you offer up for debate or reflection. You obviously want to analyse what people are saying as a result, who they're saying it to and why they're saying it. Most importantly, though, you'll need to listen. Listening is the most important thing that any brand can do to prepare for, manage and learn from attacks. In fact, it's the most important thing it can do when it's not under attack, too.

Brands aren't real, they exist in people's minds, but given they need to engage in conversation they must follow the same rules as human beings. In this case, that means using your gob and your lugholes in proper proportion: you have two ears and one mouth.

The value of these tests – and you should consider a series of minor problems as well as something weightier – is that they allow you to tinker with the defences and work out where you should be building your walls higher. You can learn a little more about where attacks may come from and how they're likely to manifest. You can sort your audience into goodies, baddies and plain average people who make up the masses. But most importantly, you can learn a lot about yourself. There is no better way to understand how the organisation will respond under pressure than to put it under a bit of controlled pressure.

It will take guts and the commitment of the brand's leaders, but it's far better than testing your mettle in the field when the snipers have you in their sights. With testing done, it's about ending the 90 days with some preparatory measures that enable the brand to be better prepared than it used to be. Not just better, but on permanent alert and with systems in place to watch the horizon, and watch the shadows.

Vigilance and diligence

If you were expecting some kind of magic formula to end this book that would give any brand superhuman protection against those that wish it ill, you're reading the wrong book. There is no magic formula. All you can do is know as much as you can about what you're dealing with, be very well prepared and have done all you can to be able to inflict counterpunches or even turn it to your advantage when you need to.

You'll be going out of the 90 days and into the wide blue yonder with a feeling of being forced to just watch and wait. That's a big part of it, of course. Being vigilant was something that you may have said you'd always been, but with the past three months behind you and systems introduced or upgraded to provide improved eyes and ears, you should have the ability to be far more comprehensive in your vigilance, having explored every corner from where threats may come.

The waiting part comes down to diligence, and not being distracted. That means ensuring that monitoring systems are employed permanently, that the communications team and senior management always know what they're doing and that clear processes are enshrined amongst those who have to act on them, just as they are for any other potential situation that involves substantial risk in any other areas of the business.

Those processes need to be joined up across all conversations, not just limited to social media or the online conversations that have been encouraged or engineered during this attempt to become match-fit. Brand vandals love to exploit not only weak spots in the brand's infrastructure, but also inadvertent or ill-advised pieces of communications that come out of the rest of the organisation. You may have the sharpest brains applied to keeping a lookout for danger and being ready to spring into action, but if your chief executive then goes and says something that's blown out of context, or commits a slip of the tongue that feels more like a slap in the face, expect any vandals wanting to wreak havoc to go there and do it.

The types of conversation that vandals will feast on are the ones borne of loose lips or moments of daftness, and to get a grip on those your vigilance and diligence needs to extend across everything that brands and its people do and say. A tall order, perhaps, but as the threats will almost certainly emerge these days in a digital form, at least they'll come in packages as ones and zeros. Which means you can track them, and you can do something about them.

It all needs to be handed off to a permanent watch. That may mean the same people being involved and all of the same systems being used. What it can't result in is a fall in standards or a lowering of the guard. There needs to be clear instruction, a detailed presentation of what has been achieved and what has been learned over the 90 days, and there need to be goals set for the function continually, not least of which must be the ability to keep pace with and ideally outsmart the techniques used by vandals to try to destroy the reputations of brands. The big attacks, the really clever ones and the cheeky ones.

And so into battle. The problem with all of this discovery, fault rectification and soul searching is that it can leave a communications team brow-beaten and discouraged. It shouldn't. You'll be in better shape to cope than you used to be.

The conversations you've begun to generate alone should be some small deterrent, perhaps, against vandalism attempts.

So what's the conclusion to all of this? A little bit of preparation goes a long way?

Well if it was as limp as that, you could be forgiven for feeling aggrieved for having forked out for this book in the first place.

Hopefully it's more constructive. Let's put it this way: the Internet is a big, fat, greasy, 'orrible sewer. And if you don't get something to keep the stench from your nostrils and some big waders to keep your feet out of the filth, you're in for a tough time. Like any sewer, it's not only highly unpleasant but there are some unspeakable things lurking in the murky depths. There is nothing, absolutely nothing, to recommend it as a pleasant experience.

Unlike being at the mercy of a sewer, constructive efforts to counter brand vandalism can offer a route out of effluent. When you're up to your neck in it you can call in the cavalry, and if you've invested time and energy beforehand, they'll come to your aid no matter what mess you're swimming in. Yes, you do need to be very well prepared, but doing so can mean you venture into the depths with a degree of confidence. And a map can help you to navigate your way out to clean air.

The keys to developing greater protection against the threat of brand vandalism, against seepage from the sewer, are the development of advocates, the development of clear systems adhered to by brave people, and the development of a better understanding of everyone the brand needs to interact with.

But besides those keys, there is one more lesson from all of this that hopefully now screams forth loud and clear.

Brand vandalism is not a game, it's a war. Know thine enemy.

INDEX

and redundancies, 81
and RSS feeds, 93
as source for journalists, 77
#WaitroseReasons, 65–6

V
value chain, impact of
    Internet on, 9
Venters, Ewan, 58, 60
Vine, 14

W
Waddington, Stephen, x, 78
Waitrose, 65–6
Walker, Howard, 51–3
Walliams, David, 15
websites, corporate, 56

whistle-blowing, 78–80
White House, the, 21–2
Wigham, Ross, 53–7
Wikipedia, 39
Wilson, Jane, 26, 202–3, 207
work–life balance, 15–16

Y
Yahoo!, 92
Yammer, 78
You Are Not a Gadget, 87
Young, Philip, 9–10
YouTube, 58–9, 63–4, 99

Z
Zeno Group, ix, 1
Zuckerberg, Mark, 33